SECRETS *of*

SELF STARTERS

48 Amazing Stories to Ignite the
Self-Starter in YOU!

Dr. Julie Miller

BOOK PUBLISHERS NETWORK

Book Publishers Network
P.O. Box 2256
Bothell • WA • 98041
PH • 425-483-3040
www.bookpublishersnetwork.com

10 9 8 7 6 5 4 3 2 1

Printed in the United States of America

LCCN 2010934499
Soft bound:
    ISBN13 978-1-935359-51-7
    ISBN10 1-935359-51-7
Hard bound:
    ISBN13   978-1-935359-61-6
    ISBN10   1-935359-61-4

Editor: Lori Zue
Cover Designer: Laura Zugzda
Typographer: Stephanie Martindale

To my beloved husband who continues to give me love, patience and support. You gave up work on your novel to be there for me. To the legacy of self-starters in my life: my grandfathers, my father, my husband, my brother and my four children.

To the self-starters profiled in this book. Without their willingness to open their hearts, their homes and their lives, this book would not have been possible. Some were colleagues, a few were friends, the majority were strangers—until now. I am humbled at their generosity, their wisdom and the incredible journeys they shared with me. They have my profound gratitude and immeasurable admiration.

CONTENTS

ONE

VISION INSPIRES POSSIBILITIES

TWO

PERSEVERANCE TRUMPS ADVERSITY

THREE
PASSION IGNITES ENERGY

FOUR
SEIZING OPPORTUNITY CAPITALIZES
ON CHANCE

FIVE

SELF-MOTIVATION DRIVES PROGRESS

SIX

CREATIVITY SPARKS SOLUTIONS

SEVEN

RISK-TAKING REAPS REWARDS

EIGHT

POSITIVE THINKING ATTRACTS POSSIBILITIES

NINE

COMPASSION ENRICHES SUCCESS

Acknowledgements

The suggestions, encouragement and good counsel received from the following people were priceless:

Big Thinking Women of Seattle, Creativity Circle, JoAnn Burgess, Dr. Lynda Falkenstein, Phyllis Grand, Barbara Hinck, Lorraine Howell, Dr. Peggy Jacobson, Dr. Mary Lynne Derrington, Rebecca Lyman, Dr. John Morford, Tammy Peniston and Dr. Carol Winkler.

Special acknowledgements

Lori Zue, my amazing editor. You made my words sing and the stories shine.

Julie Hollinger Pascal, for her critical and artistic eye with my book cover.

Dr. Lee Smith, for her editing and guidance in creating the KeyNotes at the end of each chapter.

Desi Goodwin, your assistance in getting this book completed is beyond, beyond.

Tammy Pinkston, thank you for your flexibility and timeliness in completing the interview transcriptions.

INTRODUCTION

In both my business and personal life, I've met many phenomenal people who have changed the world—or at least their corner of it. The majority of them were not born with a silver spoon in their mouth, so how is it they've achieved amazing things when so many other people in similar situations haven't?

Clearly, they possess attitudes and traits that have helped propel them to the top of their game—and nine traits, in particular, bubbled to the top when I interviewed the people featured in this book. What I also discovered is they are not so different from you and me, *except* they took action. Basically, they started. They used their own combination of attitude and a winning trait—their *traititude*—to move forward.

Whether or not you consider yourself a self-starter at this point, this book will inspire, motivate and empower you. I am passing on the wisdom of real people who found that spark. The people profiled in this book figured out what would work for them. Their stories act as exemplars so you can achieve your dreams, your goals.

As you read, perhaps you will feel affirmed and say, *I'm on my way!* You may discover a trait or an attitude you need to develop to lead a fulfilling life. If so, develop your own *traititude*. Draw on tools and skills you already have to reach the next level and ignite the self-starter in you.

Maybe you say to yourself: Why would I *want* to be a self-starter? I'm pretty happy where I am. It's the "pretty happy" part that can wear you down. I am not suggesting you drop everything and launch your own mini-conglomerate or a new non-profit. I'm saying to look at the current circumstances of your work life and find out what really motivates you. That's where you want to be, where you want to focus and excel. That's where your potential is utilized towards the goals you want to achieve and the life you want to lead.

What would ignite your *traititude* so you can express your true gifts and reach—or go beyond—your potential? How will you get what you want out of life? No worries if you don't have an immediate answer, although I bet you'll have several ideas by the time you finish this book.

Every one of these amazing people faced trials, tribulations and failure, as well as success. But all of them went for it—damn the torpedoes and full speed ahead.

Some were motivated by passion, recognition, self-expression; others were driven by their dreams. A few came from privileged backgrounds; most pulled themselves up by their bootstraps. Some experienced very rugged childhoods; others did not. Some were highly educated; others were not. Some were first-generation Americans; others were not. You will find in this book people from all walks of life, all ages and ethnicities. They all have one thing in common: they're self-starters.

THE PROFILES

THE INTRAPRENEURS, THE ENTREPRENEURS AND THE ACADEMICIANS, THE BIG HEARTS AND THE PUBLIC SERVANTS

I divided the people I interviewed into three groups. First were the intrapreneurs—those who succeeded within corporations. They saw opportunities and worthwhile risks, and they rose to the occasion, most often not waiting for permission. The second group was the entrepreneurs. They ignited their own self-starter sparks but not without spending some time honing their skill sets and absorbing everything they could before striking out on their own. The third group consists of those who work in the worlds of academia, non-profit or public service. They managed to shine in environments where status quo and safety dominate.

HERE'S WHAT YOU CAN LEARN

The nine traits presented in this book reside in these self-starters in different ways. Like you, all were born with innate talents and, for some, it was simply a matter of uncovering those gifts and combining them with motivation. Other self-starters describe how they used rocky experiences to help clarify a vision or fuel an inner drive. Others studied and developed habits they believed they lacked; they practiced and acquired their desired traits through discipline and hard work.

Read their stories, learn from their successes and failures, laugh at their anecdotes, feel encouraged by what they've overcome, celebrate their hard-won achievements.

So what kind of self-starter are you?

DESTINY IS NOT A MATTER OF CHANCE; IT IS A MATTER OF CHOICE; IT IS NOT A THING TO BE WANTED FOR; IT IS A THING TO BE ACHIEVED.

WILLIAM JENNINGS BRYAN

EVERY MORNING IN AFRICA, A GAZELLE WAKES UP.

IT KNOWS IT MUST RUN FASTER THAN THE FASTEST LION OR BE KILLED.

EVERY MORNING A LION WAKES UP.

IT KNOWS IT MUST OUTRUN THE SLOWEST GAZELLE OR IT WILL STARVE TO DEATH.

IT DOESN'T MATTER WHETHER YOU ARE A LION OR A GAZELLE.

WHEN THE SUN COMES UP, YOU BETTER START RUNNING.

OLD AFRICAN PROVERB

ONE

VISION INSPIRES POSSIBILITIES

Vision: Intention or aim; idea; farsightedness; power of imagination; mode of seeing or conceiving; dream.

A vision arrives in a flash of inspiration or builds gradually, painstakingly, with focus and attention. Visions are as immediate and relevant as the next step or as long-term and luminous as a lifetime goal. Once conceived, a vision inspires a fervent conviction, which shapes the course that has been chosen.

Living Her Dream to House the Homeless

Susan Camerer

Position: Executive Director, Vision House | **Accomplishment:** Co-Founded seven homeless facilities in greater Puget Sound, Washington | **Birthplace:** WA

Susan Camerer used to have trouble holding onto a job. She was fired from Baskin-Robbins for trying to feed the hungry, fired from a health club because of her supposedly poor leadership skills; even the small business she started with her husband didn't realize its potential.

All for the best, as it turns out, because Susan had a flash of inspiration after she and her husband, John, watched a television movie in 1989 about a homeless woman with a child. "It was nothing extraordinary—no bright lights, no wind blowing, no doors opening," she explained, "but I suddenly felt a very strong impression that I had to make a difference for the homeless in the community. That feeling just wouldn't go away."

That image of the young woman wouldn't leave Susan's mind either. "I was so moved by this story. At the time, I was a new mother, and my baby boy was at home, warm and nestled in his own crib. I feel all mothers should be able to have that same sense of security. We knew that God called us to this work; to minister to homeless mothers and their children."

Susan and her husband immediately began working on a life mission that has lasted over twenty years. They started with a homeless program for men, and built programs from there.

Susan recalled that, four years later, "I started feeling it was time for our original vision—working with homeless mothers and children—to come to life." Susan launched her new organization, called Vision House, with just a name and a prayer.

Because of the success they'd already had with the men's programs, the phone rang right away. "I would hold my own baby on my hip as I answered the phone, hearing women pleading, desperate for housing. We had to turn them down because no actual facility existed," Susan said. "Women would call day after day with babies crying in the background."

So, in 1993, they started with a double-wide mobile home provided by HUD. The cost? One dollar per year. At the end of five years, Susan knew they would need more resources to grow the program, starting with a building.

"We went to our church and asked, 'Who can help?'" Together, Susan and her husband, along with many volunteers from local churches, built a new home for Vision House piece by piece. "It was an old fashioned barn-raising. We would raise a little money, pour the concrete, raise a little money and do the framing."

Susan knows her dream would never have been achieved without her original vision. "Seeing the vision of how you can accomplish something is what makes that something possible."

Sometimes her vision was hard for others to grasp. She would speak about the future as if the vision was already realized. "I think that stressed people out because the building was in draft form and I was already placing the furniture," she chuckles.

Before the furniture could reach its new home at her facility, however, Susan faced many other obstacles. Besides money worries, issues surrounding that first building never ceased: they faced everything from warped sub-floors to stolen copper wiring, from problems with transients to problems with volunteers.

"Didn't I tell you I was stubborn?" she joked. "People would tell me no and I'd say, 'Oh yeah, well, I'll show you! I won't let go of my dream.'" She taught herself how to build a house from reading children's books. "I didn't know a joist from a hammer at first, but I learned!"

She also worked right alongside the volunteers, and sometimes by herself. One event, in particular, stands out. "I remember the cold. I remember framing in the pitch black, freezing cold, with no other volunteers—just me. I would sing praise songs to God really loud because I was scared to death, alone there on the site. It was so dark."

Throughout the building process, she was constantly tested on her tenacity and focus on her vision. "One Friday night that autumn, my husband called me at home. He said, 'You better get down here, the guys with the borer are ready to pull off the job.'" Susan shook her head and added, "I had just bought them pizza to try and keep them happy!"

As she drove back to the site a large maple leaf fell onto her windshield—an obvious reminder that winter was not far off. "I became angrier than I have ever been. It just welled up inside of me. I knew if we didn't finish digging the sewer, the project would be held up for months!"

Susan drove the rest of the way to the facility in a rage. "I arrived, and a bunch of burly construction guys with all the big equipment were taking off their gloves and starting to pack up. I reached the superintendent, grabbed his arm and said, 'It's cold out here. Do you see the leaves starting to change? We need to get this place open 'cause there are moms and kids sleeping in cars.' He put his gloves back on and started yelling at the crews, 'Let's get busy!'"

Since starting their first facility in 1990 in Snohomish County, Washington, Susan's efforts have helped nearly 700 men, women and children in their struggle to escape homelessness, poverty and abuse.

Vision House operates seven facilities, a small community center, and a childcare center for 120 children.

Twenty years later, Susan's going strong. Each autumn she still scans the sky for falling maple leaves, but worries a little less when she does see those harbingers of harsh weather. After all, she knows her Vision House is keeping hundreds of people warm, dry and safe every night.

Combining Vision With Action

Photo by Tim Pearson

Jack Canfield

Position: CEO, The Canfield Training Group | **Accomplishment:**
125 million *Chicken Soup for the Soul* books sold in 40 languages |
Birthplace: Fort Worth, TX

Jack Canfield figured it all out when he was six years old.

"I wanted to do the things I wanted to do; have the things I wanted to have. So I went about making that happen," he said with great aplomb. His philosophy—create a vision and then make it happen—frames how Jack lives his life. Today, he is known by millions of people around the world because of his widely recognized book series, *Chicken Soup for the Soul*, and his motivational programs.

Jack views a self-starter as someone who has a vision and acts on it. "A lot of people wait around for someone else to create the game, and then they're willing to play. They'll play football, for example, but don't ask them to start a team." He added, "Making your vision a reality can happen within a job or by starting something on your own."

As a young boy, Jack started something on his own when he saw an opportunity to make money hauling drinking water from the village pump to elderly ladies' houses. "I became seriously wealthy for a seven-year-old," he laughed. Jack evolved his beliefs about success and personal transformation during a series of serendipitous jobs after graduation from Harvard University in 1966 as he moved from teaching in inner-city high schools to developing curriculum for experimental colleges to presenting W. Clement Stone's Positive Mental Attitude workshops around the country.

With that compounded knowledge, Jack developed his own workshop content, grew his knowledge base with courses in such topics as psychological education, Gestalt therapy, motivation, and self-esteem. Then he tested his ideas and theories at the workshops and speeches as he worked for Insight Training Seminars, a non-profit educational organization that focuses on teaching strategies that improve personal and professional performance.

By 1983, these experiences had sufficiently gelled into key concepts and beliefs that he successfully taught to others, so Jack started his own company, The Canfield Training Group, which he still heads today.

"The main thing, as I look back over my work history, is that when I wanted something, I just went for it." Jack counts both his father and stepfather as role models. "They always went for it. They didn't always win and, in fact, sometimes they fell flat but they always tried. They really inspired me."

Jack's life purpose and vision is to inspire others to achieve their highest vision. "That purpose is important to me; without it, there would be nothing to sustain any of us through the rejections and the difficult times," he said.

He never wavered from that belief, even in the face of great resistance and struggle. The success story of the *Chicken Soup* books exemplifies this attribute.

In 1991, Jack had a brainstorm. What if he compiled into a book all the stories he had heard during the hundreds of personal development workshops he had led? Would people read them? Jack knew the stories, written by everyday people, would inspire readers to achieve their own highest vision and to remain strong in the face of adversity. Teaming with business colleague Mark Victor Hansen, the two men compiled 101 motivational short stories for the first *Chicken Soup for the Soul* book. The authors traveled to New York and pitched the book at eight meetings a day for three days. No go. No one was interested.

Next, they tried the annual Book Expo America trade show and went to hundreds of publishers' booths with their spiral-bound notebook of stories in hand. No go. In all, 144 rejections.

Then, by chance, a small publishing firm, Health Communications, Inc., decided to take a leap of faith on the book concept.

Unfortunately, the books did not fly off the shelves, so Jack and Mark decided to visit a spiritual guide. From that session, the two men promised each other they would follow the "Rule of Five"—five activities every day to achieve their vision, which was to have a bestselling book. The rule was based on an allegory the guide had shared: "If you go to a tree with an ax and take five swipes each day, the tree, even a redwood will eventually come down."

They did radio shows, gave speeches, sent out five free books, scheduled interviews, wrote articles and press releases—they even gave books to the jurors in the O.J. Simpson trial. Despite these daily, consistent efforts, the first *Chicken Soup* book still took fourteen months to hit the bestseller list. "After that, it was like a runaway freight train," he said.

Jack never gave up on the vision that these stories would inspire and motivate millions of people and give hope to still others. "My vision sustained me. I felt the need for this book—passionately—and did not allow myself to be deterred." Including that original book, 225 titles have generated more than 125 million books sold. At one point, "we had set the *Guinness Book of World Records* for having seven books on the *New York Times* bestseller list on the same day," he chuckled.

His steadfast vision to help and inspire others remains strong. His company works with organizations and individuals all over the world, showing them how to "get from where you are to where you want to be."

In 2004, Jack started the Transformational Leadership Council, which is a group of thought leaders, speakers and authors in the fields of personal and professional development. The Council's focus is to enhance their members' effectiveness as well as make a contribution to the world. "I wanted to connect all the people who were doing personal transformational work together because there is synergy in meeting with peers." Through this council, he continues his lifelong passion for learning and further solidifies his vision: Showing people how to create a vision and make it happen.

Visionary Sleeps Well With Self-Built Empire

Sunny Kobe Cook

Position: Keynote speaker and business consultant; Founder of the Kobe Foundation | **Accomplishment:** Rose from Kelly temp to Founder/CEO of a $50 million company | **Birthplace:** Kansas City, KS

Sunny Kobe Cook, beautifully dressed and coifed, is undeniably the queen of mattresses. She exemplifies how you make dreams your reality. "I believe the definition of a self-starter is having a picture—a vision—in your head and a belief in your heart about what your life will become."

That picture took Sunny from being a "Kelly Girl" temp worker to the founder and CEO of Sleep Country USA, a company with over $50 million in sales in 28 locations and a franchise of 80 stores across the U.S. and Canada.

Sunny carried an image in her head of what she wanted to become— an extraordinarily interesting person. "I knew my life was going to be exceptional. I knew I was going to travel the world, see things my family had never seen, do things that normal people didn't do on a regular basis—that was going to be my life."

You would have never guessed it if you met Sunny as a pre-teen. She was introverted, shy, with a "stupid kinky perm and sturdy shoes." She had an unhappy school life with few friends. "I had just a horrific experience from kindergarten through eighth grade. I was a major dork, deeply depressed, and mercilessly teased."

But the butterfly emerged when Sunny left the rigidity of Catholic school to attend public high school. Sunny said to herself, "This is my chance. These new kids don't know I'm a geek. When I walk through that door I'm going to be a different person."

Sunny decided she would change everything about herself—from her clothes to her personality to even her handwriting. "I created a fictional character in my head and gave her all the attributes that I wanted to have but didn't believe I possessed, including being outgoing, and someone who tried new things. Now, mind you, this was in the head of a fourteen-year-old, so it was pretty shallow at the time." But the new persona gave her confidence and gained her friends. She joined groups, participated in clubs and was voted by the student body to give the commencement keynote address.

After high school, Sunny's college plans derailed when her parents divorced and their assets were frozen. So, in 1976, she started her career at Kelly Services, Inc., which placed her in temporary positions with other companies. "I did that on purpose because I didn't know what I wanted to do. I knew this would give me experience in lots of companies." It was a good plan and led to permanent employment with a local insurance agency. All was going well until Sunny was fired. "Let's say it was a difference of opinion," she says, blank-faced.

"I lost that job and didn't know how I was going to pay the rent. But I believe in divine intervention. My sister called and she'd heard of a job opening through her connections." And with those connections, Cook interviewed and was hired into the secretarial pool at Moore Business Forms. "I had to take a typing test. I said to myself, 'Oh, God, I hate timed typing tests. This is not my strength!'"

Just as she put her fingers to the keys, someone from the company came in the room and announced that because the company had recently secured a contract with the state of Kansas, which viewed timed tests as discriminatory, the company would no longer require these tests either. "This is the only time I was really glad that liberals were running things!" she laughed. She worked at that company for ten years, earning several promotions and "opportunities to stretch my wings and do things well beyond my job description."

But Sunny had a vision, an idea rumbling around in her head—to start her own retail business selling just one product: mattresses. "I loved retail, especially home furnishings. I realized that in the furniture world, mattress sales often keep the doors open. It requires less cash up front, it's not so fashion-responsive, and it's easier to execute than a full-line store. It was a natural fit for me."

In 1991, she put together a cost analysis plan on a little Brother word processer and met with the CFO of Simmons on several occasions. "He would throw scenarios at me. I would go home and work out different configurations and start typing. Back then, it took hours to print reports, so I would go to sleep and the next morning a new set of numbers would be ready to show to him."

Finally he said, "Okay, we're going to do this with you because we think you will be successful. Can you open in Seattle?"

Sunny spent two straight weeks checking out her Seattle competitors. "I gathered notes, took pictures and got thrown out of a couple stores."

In June 1991, with $5,000 in hand from a modest inheritance, Sunny opened her first store and named it Sleep Country USA. Within a year, she had eight stores, then a total of thirteen in the second year, and then franchises in Canada. In the 1990s, her company was the first retailer in the United States to be recognized as the "Best Place to Work," by *Washington CEO* magazine and she was named "Northwest Woman Entrepreneur of the Year" by *Inc.* magazine in 1993.

As her business grew, Sunny gave back to the community—mattresses for the homeless, a camp for at-risk youths, artistic productions for homeless children. She also started the Kobe Foundation, which provides grants to groups and individuals that focus on self-reliance, personal accountability and hard work. One hundred percent of her book profits reside in the foundation. And, not surprisingly, she's also internationally recognized for her charitable giving.

In 2000, Sunny sold Sleep Country USA and started work on her new vision of her life: to write a book, become a speaker, travel, and focus on her Kobe Foundation. In a few short years, she became a celebrated author, sought-after keynote speaker, and business consultant. And those places she wanted to go? Well, she's been to all seven continents at least twice and she's still traveling.

"To me, self-starters don't necessarily have a plan on how to achieve their vision but the picture is clear in their minds. As a result, actions they take every single day get them closer. For a poor girl from Kansas City with my background," she smiled, "my vision was considered audacious. But I didn't know any better."

TELLING STORIES THAT NEED TO BE TOLD

MICHAEL DAVIE

Position: Freelance documentary filmmaker | **Accomplishment:** Emmy Award-winning documentarian | **Birthplace:** Zimbabwe

"I wanted to get my ass kicked by life," Michael Davie explained passionately.

His wish was granted when Michael was arrested in Mozambique in 1997 with no passport, no journalism permit, no ability to contact his embassy, and no one who knew he was in the country. The ass-kicking generated a jail cell epiphany and a stunningly clear vision for his life.

Zimbabwean-born documentary filmmaker Michael Davie is an Emmy Award winner who tackles some of the world's biggest problems in the toughest locations on the planet. From Morocco to Peru to the Congo, Michael captures stories that must be told.

Michael grew up in a country town in Australia where he emigrated at a young age with his parents; all three were refugees from the civil war in Rhodesia (modern-day Zimbabwe). As a child, Michael knew he was competitive, but had never needed to rely on that attribute within the confines of a school.

"At age 15, I transferred to a new high school and was put in a class with all these brainy kids. I felt a little out of my depth; all of them were working hard and competing. So in response, I overcompensated: I wanted to prove to the world that I could do something."

Michael looked to his father for a role model. "My dad—a doctor— was such an incredible person. He saved many lives during the civil war in Zimbabwe. He also ran a refugee camp in Zaire for hundreds of thousands who had escaped the genocide of Rwanda. I wanted to be incredible too." Although he did not yet have a clear vision of his future, he knew it would be big and bold.

While in college, Michael worked on creating that bold vision. "I was very driven. I wanted to be a writer, a playwright, and an actor." None of those career choices panned out for him; the only job he could find after graduation was that of journalist at a small regional television station in rural Australia.

"I spent eight months up to my knees in cow dung, writing stories about Bob-the-banana-farmer's new tractor, or about Sue, who won the chickpea festival, or how many head of cattle sold that week. Not real thrilling stuff for a young bloke like me . . . although I did have a role in a really bad Japanese commercial!"

Through all the daily, mundane aspects of his life, he always had a vision of experiencing life on a grand scale. He just didn't yet know what that experience would look like, or what would come of it.

"I was bored with the television journalist job. My stories were not setting the world on fire. I wanted to find something big to write about."

Michael's dream of having a writing and film career got off to a slow start, especially after a promised job teaching English literature in his home country failed to materialize after he had already made his travel plans. Lying in bed one night, knowing he had a one-way, non-refundable ticket to Africa on his dresser, he had an idea.

He decided to hitchhike from Cape Town, at the southern tip of Africa, to Cairo, on the continent's northern edge, and videotape his experience. "I said to myself, 'well, I know how to write, I know a bit about television, film and telling stories, and I have $15,000 in the bank.' I pitched it to Australian Broadcasting Corporation (ABC), and told them, 'I will put all my money on the line to make this documentary.' They said, 'Well, if you survive the trip and come back with footage that's any good, we'll match your $15,000 investment.' So, off I went."

Michael's vision truly came into focus on that fateful day in Mozambique as he sat in a holding cell—panicked and without resources—after being snatched off the streets by the police because he filmed a segment on land mine victims.

He had an epiphany that day.

Suddenly the life vision he'd long sought was crystal clear. Thinking about the five-year-old girl whom he had just filmed as she learned to walk with a crude prosthetic provided the answer to a question he hadn't known he was asking.

Michael now knew exactly what he wanted to do, who he was and what he wanted to achieve. He promised himself that if he got out of that jail, he would devote his skills and talents to "telling the stories of people who don't have a voice, people who have courage and strength that we can learn from, people whose stories deserve to be told."

Luckily, Michael was released from jail the same day and then kicked out of the country. The result?

He made four half-hour documentary films about his experience. They were distributed worldwide and eventually sold to National Geographic Television. In 1999 he was invited to make documentaries for the National Geographic Society.

Since then, Michael has written, directed and produced films on such topics as the execution-style slaughter of rare mountain gorillas, a prison choir in South Africa, a medicine hunter in Peru, and terrorism in Morocco. He has risked his life to make films about the violent abuse of women in Pakistan, the plight of war refugees in the Balkans, and the child soldiers in Africa. All of Michael's documentaries are riveting stories crafted by an Emmy Award-winning master, whose mighty vocation stems from an illuminating vision for his future.

Michael never lost sight of what he wanted to achieve; he knows you have to "be patient and persistent to achieve your dreams."

Though his original motivation and dream was to "be famous, to be on television, to make a mark, to show all those really smart kids who beat me on high school exams that I was capable of doing something unusual and extraordinary," he discovered something else. "My motivation became more layered. It became more about the importance of what my project could do for others.

"As a self-starter, I let go of the idea that *I* was the journey. Instead, I let the journey take me, and I remain open-hearted."

Dream It, Then Do It

Stephanie Himonidis

Position: Radio/Television Personality | **Accomplishment:** Emmy Award winner; one of the most popular deejays in regional Mexican radio, Univision Radio, KSCA *La Nueva* 101.9 FM | **Birthplace:** Guadalajara, Mexico

"I've always dreamed I would be somebody. And everything I have dreamed so far has come true!" smiled Stephanie Himonidis.

This petite young Mexican woman radiates spunk and ambition. Born and raised in Guadalajara, Mexico, Stephanie transformed herself into the hottest "It Girl" on Spanish radio in America. She's known as "Chiquibaby," one of the most popular deejays in Los Angeles.

"I always wanted to be a television or radio personality, but a smart one." Her path, unfortunately, was laid out for her as she grew up in Mexico, which was far from the bright lights of Los Angeles' entertainment industry. Her family believed she would be a doctor, like her father. "I held the medical school application in my hand and, sadly, turned to my parents and said, 'I can't do this. I want to study communications.'"

"My mother scoffed, 'You just want an MMC,' which is a Spanish acronym for *MIENTRAS ME CASO,* a 'getting-married degree,'" she laughed, "but eventually they came around and supported my decision."

By chance, while studying communications at the Universidad de Guadalajara, Stephanie interviewed at a radio station and in 1999 became the "new voice of Super Stereo" at Nucleo Radio Guadalajara. A year later she met a representative from CBS and landed a deejay job for a Spanish-speaking radio station playing a pop format (CBS Radio's VIVA 106 FM) in Fresno, California. "I was twenty years old and moved from the cosmopolitan city of Guadalajara to the small town of Fresno. I had this spikey personality and I came with a vibe. In Fresno, I had to completely change my message and learn to talk to the people in that community—many of whom were farmers and probably illegal. But it was great—I was so motivated! I wanted to use my words to empower people, especially women, to become whatever they wanted to be."

Stephanie was flying high until the radio station changed its format and she was out of a job. She then became a spokesperson for an auto dealership—"for old, used cars"—and she was miserable.

"My dream, where was my dream?!" she asked herself at that point, knowing she had strayed from the vision she'd long held—and had actually lived for several years.

Through contacts, in 2004 she was offered a deejay (on-air talent) job at Univision Radio in San Diego (VIVA 102.9 FM), the largest Spanish-language radio broadcaster in the United States. "I think my career taught me a life lesson. To reach your dreams, you have to give up things," she said. "I gave up my boyfriend, my family and moved to another city all alone. And I was okay with that."

Self-starters, she believes, are dreamers who wake up every day with a goal, a purpose of how to achieve that dream. "All my big dreams have put butterflies in my stomach, which is a sign that I have to go for it. I've been afraid and felt insecure, but my dreams have given me the power to become who I am and who I want to become."

To restart her career in the pop music genre, she worked the night shift. "I was bored and I needed to do something during the day so I applied to be a reporter on Univision Television. Instead, I landed a job as a morning host. So there I was, Chiquibaby on the radio, and interviewing to be a serious newscaster on television in the early morning—one of my major dreams!"

In 2008, at age 26, she received two Emmys for her work on how beauty—or the lack thereof—impacts women. She also appeared on Univision Network's *Viva el Sueño* (*Live the Dream*), and *Despierta San Diego* (*Wake Up San Diego*).

Meanwhile, her nighttime radio gig at Univision's VIVA 102.9 FM flipped genres and she was back to playing oldies. No more Chiquibaby. So she returned to her roots and worked in regional Mexican stations based out of San Diego.

Finally, in 2008, she ran into a representative from Univision, "who said five magical words to me: 'the L.A. gig is open.' " Stephanie landed the job, left her boyfriend, and moved to Los Angeles to work in the No. 1 market in Spanish-language radio in America. "I was Chiquibaby once again!"

Besides her midday radio show on KSCA *La Nueva* 101.9 FM playing regional Mexican music, she does product endorsements in Spanish for major companies.

As she achieves her dreams, her vision of the future evolves. She says soberly, "I really want to become that woman who stands in the stadium and talks to girls about dreaming; about becoming what they want. Not just having a pay stub every month, but doing what you dream about. And to follow your dream you have to be the best, do your best. You have to work hard.

"I wanted to be a newscaster, so I became a newscaster. I wanted to be in the No. 1 market—L.A.—and now I have proven I could do this to myself and to others, who didn't believe I could make it.

"There are still a lot of things I want to pursue, but I have to dream them first," Stephanie says energetically.

Soaring High With a Clear End Goal

Debra Facktor Lepore

Position: President, AirLaunch LLC; President, DFL Space, LLC |
Accomplishment: First woman to run a Russian-based American aerospace corporation; Lead Engineer for Congressionally-mandated Space Launch Modernization Plan | **Birthplace:** MI

Debra Facktor Lepore's unusual blend of entrepreneurialism and aerospace engineering began when she dressed up as an elf during the Christmas season in 1982.

"That costume was my first fashion statement," Debra winked, as she explained how she worked in a Detroit mall during high school helping kids send letters to Santa on the computer. Since her boss didn't know a thing about computers—but Debra and her father did—she set up the database for the company. "That was my first entrepreneurial job!" she joked.

Debra has always had that entrepreneurial spirit. Early on during her busy, high-achieving childhood, she envisioned her life. "I wanted to do things that had never been done before," she said proudly.

23

During a high school career day, she thought, "'I like math and science, so I could be a doctor, like my dad' . . . but I didn't like blood. So then I thought, 'well, I'll be a dentist' . . . but I didn't like bad breath. 'Well, maybe I'll be an engineer,' was my next bit of logic."

She sat in on a presentation by the Society of Women Engineers, and thought, "This is way too boring." But while wandering the halls of the career day event, she saw a brochure for an aerospace company.

Intrigued with the topic, she decided to do a high school project on the space shuttle. She called the University of Michigan's aerospace engineering department and asked if she could interview faculty members. Then she listened to a student lecture on flying a spacecraft to Mars.

"I turned to my mother and said, 'Well, this is what I'm going to do. I want to be head of NASA, get my undergrad in aerospace engineering, and my MBA in strategic planning.' And that's how I came up with my plan."

Looking back, it's apparent Debra planned her work and—for the most part—worked her plan. Her chosen path incorporated her love of space exploration and her strategic thinking abilities. She was accepted at all the colleges where she applied, and got the internships she wanted—at General Motors, working on automobiles, and at McDonnell Douglas, working on fighter jets. It wasn't exactly outer space, but she gained skill sets that were advantageous later.

Even with multiple attractive job offers after receiving her bachelor's of science from University of Michigan in 1988, she understood she needed impressive technical credentials to succeed in a man's world. So Debra began her master's program in aerospace engineering at University of Michigan and completed the two-year program in one year.

"I wouldn't advise that for anyone. You have no life. But I'd made up my mind to just do it and get out of there. Essentially, I don't remember much of that entire year," Debra smiled ruefully.

Her career mirrors her definition of a self-starter. "A self-starter has ideas and goes with them. She doesn't worry about what the rules are or what you're supposed to do. When you're a self-starter, you have a vision and an end goal, and you figure out ways around the excuses you might get from others or the obstacles you might confront. You see the links between things. I call it being clever."

She cautioned, "You also have to work to execute your ideas, because some of the very best ideas don't happen without forward movement."

Debra remained keen on working with rockets. She was invited to work for the think tank ANSER—experts in planes and space—in Washington, D.C., which kept her focus razor sharp and moving along with her life's plan. Her abilities to understand the technical aspects of rockets and also see the big picture served her well.

While at ANSER, she helped form an entrepreneurial venture within the company, named the Center for International Aerospace Cooperation. "I knew about Russian engines and space policy, and others knew about systems engineering, so we partnered with Russia—the former enemy—on a project."

That project positioned her as Chief of Moscow Operations for ANSER's Center for International Aerospace Corporation. "In 1992, at the end of the Cold War, we opened an office in Moscow, but I wasn't allowed to go for two years because I was young and female—an obstacle that did not stand in the way of my vision."

This opportunity opened doors for Debra; doors beyond the United States and beyond space transportation. "The position in Moscow gave me credibility and built my reputation, and it also allowed me to become a Fellow with the International Women's Forum Leadership Foundation."

She has put to good use her unique skill set of business acumen, technical skills and how to develop and follow a strong vision. Though her vision changed slightly when she decided not to pursue her MBA, she earned her business credentials on the job with eight years at a startup, including two as vice president of Business Development and Strategic Planning, at Kistler Aerospace Corporation, based in Kirkland, Washington.

Debra also didn't end up running NASA like she had originally planned, but she has many other accomplishments under her belt: she's worked with the U.S. Air Force, the White House Office of Science and Technology, the National Space Council, the Ballistic Missile Defense

Organization and numerous other entities. She and her colleagues have worked on such projects as human spaceflight, alternative launch concepts for defense systems, and commercial space launch systems.

In the mid-1990s she was lead engineer for the Congressionally-mandated Space Launch Modernization Plan, and she contributed to the ten-year Space Launch Technology Plan. She is in her third term on the U.S. Department of Transportation's Commercial Space Transportation Advisory Committee and is president of the Women in Aerospace Foundation. She most recently ran Air Launch LLC, the developer of the QuickReach™ small-launch vehicle.

On her accomplishments, Debra reflected, "You know, I think it's really interesting that I grew up outside of Detroit, the car capital, and I thought cars were so boring, but I ended up in transportation anyway. I guess I just wanted to go faster, farther, and do stuff that was different."

Vision and Discipline: An Unbeatable Pair

Jon Robertson

Position: Conductor, Redlands Symphony Orchestra; Dean, Conservatory of Music, Lynn University, Boca Rotan, Florida | **Accomplishment:** First African-American to receive master's and doctorate degrees from Julliard School of Music | **Birthplace:** Jamaica

A child prodigy at the piano by the time he was six, Jon Robertson debuted in 1951 at age nine in New York's Town Hall to rave reviews—this young Jamaican's career was now in the major leagues.

For this self-starter, two attributes—vision and discipline—work hand in glove. Jon defines vision as the desire to achieve a dream. The dream is the "deep essence" that fans the flame, and ignites the spark within, he explained. And discipline? Well, that's another matter.

"There are people who have the desire—the vision—but they don't have the discipline," he said, describing how the two attributes are symbiotic. "These people self-start a thousand different things that never reach fruition because they don't have the discipline to weather the inherent storms that come along.

"When you come from a West Indian family, discipline is a very, very, very real part of life," said Jon. That discipline—"doing well what you don't want to do at all"—propelled him to the peak of musical heights. "You can have exceptional opportunities come your way, but without discipline you cannot succeed."

Jon's schooldays had their challenges. With all his concertizing, he had no time to attend regular high school. "Because I was black, finding a tutor to help me complete my high school studies was nigh on impossible. Someone finally took me on after hours. That way, the other clients wouldn't see me coming into the building." He shrugged, with no hint of bitterness. "Oh, yeah, that's just how it was in the '50s."

At high school graduation, Jon received a six-year scholarship to Juilliard School of Music for undergraduate studies. After Juilliard, he became the youngest chairman of a music department at an accredited university—Oakwood College in Huntsville, Alabama.

While there, an opportunity presented itself that launched Jon into what became his true calling. He was asked to choral conduct the *Verdi Requiem* with the university's choir. With critical acclaim for his conducting from both the *Los Angeles Times* and the *New York Times,* he mused, "I guess it was an indicator to me that maybe I had some talent.

"I had caught the conducting bug. It was like a terminal illness: once you get it, it won't let you go." He turned down a prestigious job as faculty member at a prominent university to pursue this dream. "This was the major decision of my life because it turned me, once and for all, in the direction of conducting." This less-traveled path did not have the "built-in securities and rest stops along the way," he recalled, "but it was divine leadership that pulled me onto this road."

So, on a dare from his wife, he applied for and was accepted into an elite conducting class with Herbert Blomstedt—one of the world's most renowned conductors—who, at the time, was also Conductor Laureate of the San Francisco Symphony. "I was afraid to apply because what if this extremely prominent man—one of the greatest conductors in the world—says to me, 'You ought to stick with the piano.'"

Instead, Jon became Blomstedt's first and only private student and traveled to Sweden to study. He eventually secured the position as conductor and music director of the Kristiansand Symphony Orchestra in Norway, and for the next decade commuted every two weeks from his home in Los Angeles to his job.

Jon's conducting career took him all over the world. But in 1987, after ten years on the road, "the commuting was getting old and my daughters needed me."

He decided to return to the academic world as Chair of the Department of Music at the University of California, Los Angeles (UCLA). During his twelve-year tenure, Jon created the Music Outreach Program, developed for inner-city African-American and Latino students. "I wanted to show others how to achieve their dream."

The program, begun in 1994, matches UCLA's music students to students enrolled in music programs at selected inner-city schools in Los Angeles. On a weekly basis, the collegians give private lessons to the younger students. Additionally, the students are tutored in math and reading in preparation for the SAT exams, thanks to a grant from the Toyota Foundation.

The results are phenomenal: Ninety-eight percent of the students in the program go on to colleges in the United States. Because of this success, Jon received the President's Award for Outreach Programs in 2004.

Presently, Jon is the dean of Lynn University's Conservatory of Music in Boca Raton, Florida. Under his visionary leadership, the conservatory joined the ranks of major conservatories and institutions of music, boasting a world-renowned faculty of performers and scholars. He has also celebrated his twenty-sixth season as the conductor of the Redlands Symphony Orchestra in southern California.

With all his successes, Jon's humility is as surprising as it is refreshing. "It's one of the things my mother instilled in me. She said to me a thousand times, 'God gave you this talent and if you get a big head, He will take it away from you. He has only lent it to you for you to share with others,'" Jon chuckled.

KeyNotes

Self-starters are vision setters. Giving yourself permission to slow down long enough so that you can move ahead with the vision you want for your life is a discipline. Really taking the time to reflect, to think, to envision your future is essential to having the life you want to lead.

Ask yourself:

1. When I think of the happiest, most satisfied time of my life, what was I doing then?

2. What is (or has been) my true purpose in life?

3. If my story were to be included in this chapter, how would it describe my vision? And what have I accomplished or achieved with that vision?

Activities:

- Write your own story by answering this question: What is my amazing story? Start with "Once upon a time, there lived . . ."

- As you responded to the questions above, your brain responded with images. Pay attention to what you see in your mind's eye. Describe or draw those images in a journal or on a piece of paper . . . or in the margins of this book!

Two

PERSEVERANCE TRUMPS ADVERSITY

Perseverance: Insistence; resolve; determination; stubbornness; doggedness; steadfastness.

This list of traits aptly describes these self-starters. They hold an absolute, unwavering devotion to their cause or their organization or their beliefs and the steady obstinacy to not give up. Their strong resolve to realize their goals keeps them moving forward.

GLOBAL AID ROOTED IN IOWA

NANCY AOSSEY

Position: President/CEO, International Medical Corps |
Accomplishment: Grew International Medical Corps from startup
organization to $150 million annual budget | **Birthplace:** Cedar
Rapids, IA

Nancy Aossey has been working—and working *hard*—since she
was a little girl. Today, Nancy runs one of the world's largest
humanitarian organizations, International Medical Corps, based in
Santa Monica, California. This non-governmental organization (NGO)
has delivered more than $1 billion in assistance and health services to
tens of millions of people in over fifty countries.

In large part thanks to Nancy's brilliant leadership, the organization
grew from just three staff members and a handful of volunteers when it
started in 1986 to a multi-national organization with an annual budget
of $150 million and 3,500 volunteers worldwide in 2009. And what is
the attribute she believes makes her a self-starter? Perseverance.

To absolutely never give up is "a biggie for me. So often people feel defeated when there's a setback, because the first time they tried something, it didn't work, so they gave up. Perseverance will take you over or under or around obstacles. Sometimes it's three steps forward, one step backward, then two steps forward again. You have to figure out the way and have the right attitude. You can't let the setbacks get in the way of what needs to be done."

For Nancy, what needs to be done is to deliver medical relief and healthcare training to some of the most violent and troubled spots in the world.

Nancy's staff and volunteers work in low-income, fragile and post-conflict regions such as Darfur, northern Uganda, the Democratic Republic of Congo, Liberia, Chechnya, Ethiopia and Iraq. "In our early days we were working in countries like Angola, Somalia and Afghanistan. These were really, really tough places. Our program's success was based on our ability to persevere, to get something done, to not let the fear of failure get in our way."

Nancy's belief that perseverance is the key attribute to success extends to those people her organization impacts. "I have seen the resilience of the human spirit. I am humbled when we are able to restore dignity to people who have persevered through unimaginable suffering."

Nancy has learned to view problems as opportunities and to see the bright side of even the darkest situations. "We were the first American-based organization to enter Somalia. There was just tremendous, tremendous grief and suffering. We figured out how to get established on the ground despite the violence; we figured out how to work with people in the community despite the fighting; we figured out how to get supplies into the country despite very rugged terrain. We did what others thought couldn't be done. And I'm telling you there were literally thousands—and I'm not exaggerating—*thousands* of obstacles. Giving up has never been an option."

Nancy has grown with the organization. In 1986, with only two years of work experience, she joined the fledgling International Medical Corps—a group of idealists with great ideas, a great mission and a great cause.

"I was twenty-seven years old, and we were very entrepreneurial. I realized this was the place for me, with people I wanted to work with and a powerful mission—to teach others how to help themselves and to rehabilitate health care and economic systems. That's what I love."

Nancy has always had a philosophy of perseverance and care for others. "My parents instilled in me a very, very strong work ethic. From a young age, I was involved with civic and community work because they strongly believed in the importance of doing our part."

As a youngster Nancy babysat, ran a lemonade stand and worked in the corn fields. "That was my favorite job—it was 150,000 degrees in the Iowa summer humidity, and I would spend my days pulling little things off the top of corn so they would grow properly!" She followed her parents' guidance and now perseveres on the world stage—often in what feels like 150,000 degrees.

Over the years Nancy has assisted numerous devastated populations, including Somalis struggling with violence and famine, Indonesians who suffered through the 2004 tsunami and Haitians during the 2010 earthquake.

Considered one of the world's top advisors on issues of humanitarian assistance and emergency medical relief, Nancy works closely with other international agencies such as the World Health Organization, UNICEF, the World Food Program and the U.S. Department of Health and Human Services. She frequently testifies before Congress and has briefed leaders in the White House—including presidents, vice presidents and first ladies—on humanitarian issues.

Pretty good for a girl who grew up in Iowa, detasseling corn.

FLYING IN THE FACE OF OBSTACLES

DAVID LOAIZA

Position: VP, Quantitative Research, JPMorgan Chase (current); White House Fellow (former) | **Accomplishment:** On the ground Technical Team Lead for nuclear negotiations with North Korea | **Birthplace:** Bolivia

How did a young man from Bolivia, who spoke no English when he arrived as a high school senior, become a technical advisor for U.S. nuclear talks with North Korea? Through persistence.

"I just put my head down and keep working. I am not concerned with failure. I just persevere," said David Loaiza as he described his phenomenal transformation.

David developed persistence at a very young age. "I came from a third-world country, and we were a family of modest means." With no mother in the house and a father who worked continuously, David had to make his own way. "My dad would provide the basics, but we didn't have much money for school supplies. Sometimes there was no money for pencils and paper, so I had to figure it out, I had to improvise." David collected office paper that had been used on one side so he could use the opposite side to copy information from the blackboard; teachers wrote complete lessons on the board since textbooks were scarce. Sometimes he even had to borrow a classmate's pencil.

Though David's family struggled, they never turned away those in need. "We were a family with four kids, with little money left over. However, my father still adopted more kids. If anybody was in trouble, they would come and live with us. My house was like a hotel. I rarely had a Christmas present, and we often went to bed hungry."

During the Bolivian hyper-inflation crisis of the '80s, the family food budget allowed for only a daily slice of bread. "A piece of bread was the greatest thing you would eat," David recalled. "The bread cupboard was locked. My father would get the key and, with great ceremony, slice the loaf of bread—one piece per person."

Not surprisingly, David faced many challenges when he arrived in the U.S. He had no family, no English language skills, and no computer proficiency. Through the goodwill and encouragement of his host family (Sanson family in New Mexico) and thanks to David's doggedness, he conquered these obstacles.

"I was determined to learn the language, so I spent a lot of time watching commercials and cartoons, so I could pick up simple words and vocabulary." He completed high school, received a scholarship to the University of New Mexico and finished his undergraduate degree. "My first semester in college was extremely, extremely difficult. Language was an issue. I didn't know how to type proficiently. Everything was so very time-consuming. But you can decide on self-pity or whining, or you can find a way to do what you want to do."

That's exactly what David did. After completing his master's of science degree in nuclear engineering, he was approached by Los Alamos National Laboratory (LANL). He worked and studied there, and completed his PhD in the same field before he was twenty-six.

His hard work and expertise in the field of reactor physics were soon recognized. In 2006, David accepted a change of station as a technical advisor for the U.S. Department of Energy Office of Nonproliferation and International Security and was brought on as an advisor for the nuclear talks with North Korea. He was thirty-six years old.

"Our job was to figure out how to perform the disablement actions in support of the talks. I understood the nuclear cycles, and since most diplomats don't have that level of knowledge, they rely on technical advisors to guide them." David helped shape the U.S. non-proliferation policy, and traveled to North Korea seven times in 15-day trips to monitor the country's denuclearization.

It was during his rotation in North Korea that another opportunity presented itself: to become a White House Fellow. This program, one of America's most prestigious, offers exceptional young men and women firsthand experience working at the highest levels of the federal government. The application process is grueling and the competition stiff, but David, however, was not deterred.

"One of the keys to my success is that I overcome obstacles. Sometimes the process is very slow before the answer becomes clear," David said.

Most people with his travel schedule would have given up. But not David. Ten essays were part of the screening process, and David wrote them while traveling to and from North Korea. "As you can imagine, there was no privacy or security. And here I was trying to write a mock memo to the president!" he chuckled.

Once he made the cut, David had to fly nearly around the clock from Korea to D.C., then land and immediately jump into a round of interviews. "I had no Internet, no ability to call anybody. I just had to dig in and do it." Once he was chosen as a finalist, the hard work intensified: more interviews, both regional and national. "At one point, I did ten interviews in two days," he said.

He landed the Fellowship. Because he wanted to broaden his repertoire of skills, David asked to work in the White House Office of Management and Budget. He was bluntly told they wanted no Fellows, but David persevered. "I wasn't going to give up on this opportunity," he said. "So, after several calls, the Placement Office finally gave me thirty minutes to sell myself. They asked, 'Why would a nuclear physicist want to work in a budget department?' I told them I was motivated, knew how to work, how to talk to people. I didn't need someone to hold my hand. The Office manager responded, 'It doesn't make any sense to hire a nuclear physicist, but all right.'"

David has never let his obstacles stand in the way of success. "Many people are three, four times more intelligent than I am, but I rely on my ability to work hard and my ability to say, 'Okay, why not me?' Nothing comes easy. But I just keep moving forward. I pride myself on not giving up, even when the odds don't look so great. I just persist."

When this book went to press, David had just accepted a job with JPMorgan Chase as vice president of Quantitative Research, where he will, undoubtedly, soar high over any obstacles he faces.

POCKET CHANGE AND MEGA-DEALS

DAVE SABEY

Position: Founder/President, Sabey Corporation, a real estate development and construction company | **Accomplishment:** Sabey Corp. is world's largest private owner of leased data center space | **Birthplace:** WA

Dave Sabey made money like most lower-middle class kids did: picking blackberries, selling pop bottles and mowing lawns, for example. But one of his biggest "cash cows" was collecting pocket change that dropped out of the pants' pockets of high school sports fans. "We lived right behind the football field. As a young kid, I would lie in bed and listen to the games. When it was an especially close game—and sometimes they'd play three nights in a row—the fans would jump up and down and their change would spill out," he laughed. "We had dug a hole under the fence and the morning after the game, we went under the bleachers and found the money lying there."

"The process to success for a serial winner is a long and arduous journey. There really is an algorithm to success," stated Dave Sabey of Sabey

Corporation. "And a big part of it is that it takes tremendous stamina to stay the course and accomplish what you start. It takes stamina to recover from multiple setbacks and lots of mistakes. It takes stamina to work seventy-to-eighty-hour workweeks. It's those '10,000 hours' that Malcolm Gladwell talks about," he said, referring to writer Gladwell's idea that the key to success is simply a matter of practicing something for 10,000 hours. This high degree of perseverance has marked Dave's long career as a real estate developer and capital investor.

Both Dave's parents worked for Boeing, and even though he was accepted at the U.S. Air Force Academy, they did not have the money to pay for his education. Instead, he accepted the football scholarship offered by the University of Washington. As Dave worked during college in the mid-'60s, he caught the construction bug. Starting at the bottom, he worked his way up the ranks of Weldwood, a division of US Plywood. The company's move to sell Weldwood was the impetus for Dave to start his own company, Berkeley Structures, Inc, in 1971. "I've really only had just one job all my life. I guess persistence pays off!" he smiled.

Dave's first real breakthrough in his career came from, surprisingly enough, jigsaw puzzles. He loved solving the problem of putting all the pieces together and transferred that doggedness to his business, to "figure out the picture that is unfolding. I always love that kind of stuff. And it was this mundane pastime that helped me cut my costs by 30 percent!" said Dave. In short, he determined that he could cut his costs by eliminating the planing step as part of the assembly of wood roof panels. "For two years, I had a great competitive advantage because no one really understood what my super sauce was," he grinned. Not surprisingly, Dave's company's soared to success soon after its launch.

Dave's puzzle-solving perseverance has seen him through the robust and lean years. He has always done what others would consider counter-intuitive. Rather than go after fancy buildings and properties, he took less attractive buildings and remodeled them or moved them to newly purchased lots. Rather than buy during the good times, he sold properties, and bought in bad times instead. He expanded his holdings by investing in apparel, retail companies and stores and even started a property management business.

But by the mid-'80s, financial troubles cropped up. This very successful entrepreneur faced mounting debt on his investments, his construction business slowed, a Soviet venture was on hold due to revolutions in the once-socialist republics, a $100 million shopping mall venture was behind schedule, and, even worse, the credit market had tightened.

But Dave's steadfastness, his unwillingness to give up and his laser-eye view of problem-solving helped him weather stormy waters and a tremendous financial hit. "You have to accept your failures and move on. But first I do everything possible to make things work, otherwise I'll spend the rest of my career—20, 30 or 40 years—revisiting it, and wondering, persisting, could I or should I have done something more," Sabey said. "For me, the self-starter is someone who isn't smart enough to know what he or she can't do, but has the confidence to find the knowledge, garner the resources and then the stamina to accomplish what they start," he said forcefully.

Today, Dave Sabey has built one of the most successful real estate development and construction companies in the country. His firm specializes in technology and health care, and in the renovation of historic Pacific Northwest buildings. Sabey Data Center Properties, a Sabey Corporation subsidiary, is the largest and oldest privately owned multi-tenant data center developer and manager on the West Coast. Sabey Corp. is also the world's largest private owner of leased data center space and controls the largest amount of sustainable, green, hydro-generated megawatts in the United States.

Perseverance is Dave's mainstay. "I always look at my goals as part of a positive process. It's much more efficient because you don't waste time worrying about some boogie man that might jump up at you. You spend your time driving towards a goal. If something negative comes up, you just knock it down."

Dave has dug a hole to the other side of the fence and emerged triumphant.

Tenacity Increases the Odds

Geoffrey Stack

Position: Managing Director/Principal, Sares-Regis Group |
Accomplishment: Manages $4 billion in real estate properties; raised
$8.4 million to fight cystinosis disease | **Birthplace:** Chicago, IL

Jeff Stack could have returned home after being wounded in 1968 during his tour of duty in Vietnam, but instead he returned to Vietnam because he had a commitment to his troops. He didn't lack tenacity when he entered the war, and he certainly gained more experience with that admirable trait by the time he came home.

Tenacity, he says, is the resolve and the persistence to see the positive, no matter what. Tenacity is what makes self-starters great.

"The road is littered with self-starters who failed. But if you are unafraid to fail and you have the strength of your convictions, you have tenacity. You've just got to be willing to continue to try and try and try again. You can't get discouraged and quit. You just have to say, 'Okay, let's start again.'" Those beliefs carried Jeff through trials and tribulations as he built his real estate development company during the last three decades.

Jeff started working at age ten and hasn't stopped yet. He graduated from Georgetown University in 1965 and, after the Marines, he continued on to Wharton School of Business. In 1972, he headed to California and accepted a job with a real estate development company. When the time was right, or so he thought, he left the company and went out on his own with a condo-conversion project.

"I thought it would be so easy to find an equity partner; just a piece of cake. Boy, was I shocked! I knocked on twenty doors and was turned down flat. I started to waiver. I thought I had made a bad mistake; this wasn't going to work and I had better give up," Jeff reflected. "But I just decided to knock on another ten doors until I found someone to listen to my idea."

Rather than a partner, Jeff was offered a job—at a quarter of what he had been making. "It wasn't much, but I went for it; we lived mostly off our savings," he said, agreeing to twenty-five percent of the profits and a larger percentage of whatever deals he could make. With that goal in mind, Jeff worked as hard as he could. He even rented a helicopter to survey forty-three perspective condo-conversion opportunities, and then visited every property. Within a five-year period, Jeff and his partner had converted over 7,000 apartments to condos.

The run ended in 1981 when interest rates soared to 21.5 percent. "At those rates, we couldn't give the property away. We had $85 million in loans and no way to pay them back." They worked out deals with the banks, sold all the units and emerged poorer but wiser.

In 1982, Jeff had another idea—to build A-quality properties for A-quality tenants. "No one believed in this concept. They said, 'Why would you do this?!' They thought us wanting to buy properties and then build the absolute best units was a huge mistake."

Once again, Jeff knocked on another twenty doors before he could find anyone willing to listen. "It was very, very hard. I was just ... fearless. I was not deterred, though I certainly had many doubts." Eventually that tenacity paid off for both Jeff and his business partner.

"In 1983, we finally found funding, and the rest is history, as they say. Since we started the company, we've done about seven billion dollars in business, with 19,000 apartments and condominiums, and 15 million square feet of commercial and industrial space."

Though the success of his career is largely due to his tenacity, Jeff's single-mindedness has never been more apparent than in his fight to find a cure for his daughter's disease, cystinosis. Since it's so rare, with only five hundred sufferers in North America, funding is very difficult. Jeff refuses to be disheartened.

"I believe you must have the tenacity to continue in spite of repeated failures. If what you've started doesn't work, you've got to pick yourself up and start over. You look at what you did, figure out what wasn't quite right, and then you get going on it again."

That philosophy holds true with the foundation, Cystinosis Research Foundation (CRF), he and wife Nancy created; they have raised more than $14 million for research and fellowships. That funding has contributed to seventy-eight ongoing studies by sixty researchers in eight countries, all in an effort to solve the mystery of this genetic disorder which causes death by age eight or nine if untreated; most patients die in their mid-to-late-twenties. As a result of the research studies funded by CRF, several breakthroughs have been made in potentially finding a cure for this devastating disease.

On her twelfth birthday in 2003, Jeff's daughter shared a secret wish with her mother. "I want to have my disease go away forever," she confided.

With Jeff Stack's perseverance, you can bet the odds are in her favor.

KeyNotes

Self-starters persevere. No one escapes life's adversity. We all have our ups and downs, our challenges, our sadnesses, our setbacks. But it's how we handle them that make us successful. Climbing into bed and pulling the blanket over your head is one option; whining is another. But self-starters redirect their attention and just keep moving forward—ignoring the naysayers and, with determination and downright tenaciousness, they accomplish their goals and realize their vision.

Ponder these ideas:

1. Ask yourself: What did I learn from a mistake? How will I do it differently next time? What opportunities did this situation create for me?

2. Think of a time when you did not give up on someone or something. How were you tenacious? What determined your stick-to-itiveness?

Activities:

- Create a mantra, or a saying, that you repeat when things look their bleakest. Make it a pep talk you repeat over and over to change your attitude and your perspective about a situation. For example, *I always find a way out of difficult situations, and the result is always positive.*

- Gather a group of wise friends and/or experienced professionals and form a group. These folks can act as your board of advisors and encourage you, give you advice or be your cheerleaders. If appropriate, do the same for them. You'll see other ways of using persistence to triumph over adversity.

THREE

PASSION IGNITES ENERGY

Passion: Fervor; ardor; enthusiasm; zeal. Intense emotion that compels action.

This attribute was mentioned often by those interviewed. They all talked about it, wept about it and live it every day.

From financially successful entrepreneurs to directors of non-profits, this emotion—more than any other—gets these self-starters up in the morning. Their zeal sees them through the hard times and propels them forward. Passion drives the self-starter no matter how many naysayers stand in their path.

An Accidental Self-Starter

John Campbell

Position: Founder/CEO, MyVetwork.com | **Accomplishment:** Created website used by 50 million people and which exclusively serves members of the military and their families; named Deputy Undersecretary of Defense for Wounded Warrior Care and Transition Policy | **Birthplace:** Brooklyn, NY

John Campbell is an accidental self-starter. "I've always been a corporate guy, generally working in large companies. This new venture has been kind of painful, as I haven't seen myself in the past as a self-starter," said John.

He still grapples with the label. "Entrepreneurs have a thousand ideas a minute. That's not me," he said modestly. That may be, but the one idea he did have now impacts 50 to 60 million people.

In 2006, John founded MyVetwork.com, the first-ever social network built for individuals in the U.S. military, whether they are active-duty, retired or a veteran. The site also assists their spouses, family and friends. It is a one-stop website where members of the military can go to connect, network and find needed information about everything from jobs to mental health assistance.

With the start of his military-oriented website, John has come full circle. He served in the Marines with distinction from 1967 to 1970 and was awarded two purple hearts as a platoon commander during the Vietnam War.

After he left the military in 1971, John began his nearly thirty-year-career in the banking industry. His experiences ranged from global head of commercial banking to country manager in South America after the Falklands War to deputy manager of a $1 billion JP Morgan building project. All were positions in which he thrived and achieved great success.

Though he loved his work in the banking industry, he wasn't passionate about it. He married his wife, Sue, in 1990, quit banking, and began working behind the scenes with Sue to organize her company's large-scale conferences and televised conversations with world-class thought leaders. "I was the guy behind the scenes. I did the technical, financial—everything that needed to be done."

But then the Iraq War began in 2003. "I felt pulled to get involved. It's hard to describe, other than I knew I should be doing something for the reconstitution of the destroyed financial system in Iraq," he said. John tried to get a job with the U.S. Treasury, but to no avail—his age was a preventing factor. Then serendipity stepped in.

"I contacted a fellow who was the Supreme Allied Commander of Europe. I said, 'Jim, I really want to do something around this war. I'm too old to go there and fight, so how can I help?' Jim said, 'Well, a lot of these guys need jobs. Can you help with that?'"

Campbell started by working one-on-one with military personnel to successfully transition them into the private sector. "It was great work and I was making a difference, but I just didn't have the scale I wanted. I realized that with more and more guard and reserve troops coming back, the support networks would soon be tapped out."

John felt compelled to do something to help all service members, not just the ones he was put in contact with. "I was passionate about getting this to happen because passion sure carries you through a lot of adversity," John said dryly. "Everyone told me that this was a bad idea, that it was never going to work. In some ways this whole experience is counter-intuitive for me. I liked commercial banking for a reason: the job had few risks, and I could analyze a situation and figure it out. But here I was, way out there; I was pushed forward by wanting to make something better for our military!"

The stories told by these soldiers harkened back to stories John heard when he was in Vietnam. One soldier said upon his return from combat that, having walked with the dead, he was now learning to live again.

Before Myvetwork.com, no single source existed where military personnel could find help for mental issues, job retraining, housing and the like when they returned home from active duty. The site also serves families of deployed personnel who are desperate to be kept apprised with up-to-date information of their loved ones.

John recalled, "I remember my mother was a basket case while I was in Vietnam. I can't believe after forty years we still have a support issue with the military families. I don't understand why they had to go to a hundred different places on the Internet to get information they need!

"So, I thought, wouldn't be great if we could develop a virtual military tent?" The timing was right for a military networking site. Social networking was just hitting its stride in 2006, and John discovered a software program that he could custom-design to build the community.

Today, U.S. military personnel can search the site and find whatever they need. Visitors form virtual discussion groups, submit blogs, post videos, develop friendships, assist each other in finding resources and jobs, and have even created businesses, all within the site's social networking.

John has heard many stories of how the site has helped military personnel and their families. "A mother of a twenty-two-year-old vet contacted us for help. Her son was returning from Iraq, and she wanted to celebrate his homecoming with a hero's welcome. She wanted this event to impact not just immediate friends and family but also the community." Through MyVetwork.com, she reached out to the Veterans of Foreign Wars, American Legion and others. She also contacted local television stations to get the word out. Her result? Three television stations shared her son's story, and "lots of people showed up—even strangers—who wanted to welcome him home. She then created a group on the site so that folks could communicate with each other. We call this a win!" he said proudly.

If it weren't for his passion, would John ever have started MyVet-work.com and ever have become an accidental self-starter?

"I couldn't do this work if I wasn't very passionate about it. Young men and women, and even older vets, really deserve what they've earned. It just doesn't seem fair that these people who are protecting us, who are fighting for our country, have to work so hard to earn the benefits that they are accorded. This isn't about throwing food stamps at them; it's not a handout. It's about building them a community."

Due to his deep passion for the subject, and despite other people's doubts, that's exactly what this accidental self-starter did: create a community, and one that's turning out to be bigger than many of the countries our military personnel protect.

Passion is a Requirement

Alexander L. Cappello

Position: Chairman/CEO, Cappello Capital Corp. | **Accomplishment:** Created fifty new Young Presidents' Organization chapters around the world; served on forty boards | **Birthplace:** Bakersfield, CA

When Alex Cappello walks into a room, all heads turn. With his startling good looks, his impeccable appearance and his 1,000-watt smile, he brightens any room.

Alex was born an entrepreneur because, he said only half-jokingly, he is a direct descendant of the Florentine Medici family. It's in his blood. "My dad was an entrepreneur, so was his dad, and so was my mom's dad, so I guess in that regard we were all chronically unemployable," he said with a twinkle in his eye. "Nobody wanted to hire us."

Like most entrepreneurs, Alex began working at a very young age. At eight years old he worked in the fields of Bakersfield, California, and by sixteen he ran his own packing crew. As a seventeen-year-old college freshman, he started an investment banking business, The

Cappello Group, in 1973. "I didn't know that what I was doing was called 'investment banking' back then, but I was launched," he said.

Thanks to two of his professors at the University of Southern California (USC), Alex landed an internship at the Small Business Administration (SBA), and within a month had persuaded two SBA clients to put him on retainer. "Boy, was I in tall cotton—as they say in Bakersfield—making two grand a month per client!" he exclaimed.

His professors quickly recognized his passion and intelligence, and after some well-placed introductions, Alex was given the opportunity to write a business plan and do financial modeling and forecasting for a start-up bank.

By his senior year he was paying for college by advising companies, giving motivational speeches and teaching private classes on how to package oneself for job interviews.

"My whole life has been a function of passion," said Alex. His credo is simple: "If you really want to find yourself, lose yourself in other people. If you really want to find purpose and passion in your life, you find it in helping other people."

Alex didn't stop there. He spearheaded The Cappello Group's efforts with a start-up investment bank in Switzerland in the late 1970s. From there, he picked up Middle Eastern and European clients, plus retired American CEOs. With this group of clients, his company took off.

Though he runs a banking corporation, Alex doesn't work just for the financial incentive. "One of the biggest misconceptions people have about those of us in finance-related fields is that it's all about making money. Sure, you like making money, but for me, staying intellectually stimulated, taking on new challenges, knowing that no two days are the same—it's demanding, it's high-risk with long hours and endless work, and you earn every dollar. It takes passion, focus and vision to sustain you.

"Passion can manifest itself as self-confidence, belief in what you're doing, and I guess everything in my life has, for me, been about doing the right thing—helping others." This philosophy was in full play during his two terms as the international chairman of Young Presidents' Organization (YPO), which brings the expertise, knowledge and experience of elite CEOs to developing countries. Alex believes fervently that doing so "raises the bar" for all.

"YPO is a force of good in the world, and as chairman I felt strongly that creating a legacy around the world was imperative." He spent enormous amounts of time traveling to developing countries, gathering the most prominent business people within these countries, and introducing them to the intimate global network that is YPO. "To bring capitalism to emerging markets in a constructive, positive way so that those countries can succeed is a good thing," Alex said with pride and conviction.

Alex understood that it was crucial to support not just emerging countries, but all YPO members with current business thinking. So he started the Global Leadership Conference for YPO members, which has blossomed into one of the most successful gatherings of premier business leaders in the world.

During his YPO tenure, Alex helped launch over fifty new chapters in such places as Dubai, Beijing, Morocco, Saudi Arabia, Portugal, Spain, Prague, Warsaw, Egypt and Russia. "It just shows you what a few people can do if they are really passionate about what they are doing," said Alex.

In 2006, Alex's extraordinary efforts were acknowledged by YPO, who named its highest global membership/leadership award after him: the Alexander L. Cappello Annual Award.

Since then, he has served on at least forty boards of banks, public and private companies, and non-profit organizations, including the Cheesecake Factory, Geothermal Resources, California Republic Bank, RAND Russia Forum, City of Hope and ALS Foundation. He guest-lectures all around the world and continues to receive numerous awards and recognitions for his generous contributions to the community.

Alex is puzzled by people with no passion. "They're like the walking dead; just going through the motions. You don't have to be the smartest or the biggest, but if you have passion for what you do, you will succeed."

Passion You Can Taste

Kathy Casey

Position: CEO, Kathy Casey Food Studios; Liquid Kitchen; President/Co-Founder, Dish D'Lish Cafés and Specialty Food Line | **Accomplishment**: One of first female executive chefs in the U.S.; early pioneer of Bar-Chef movement | **Birthplace**: WA

"My first professional cooking gig was for nuns," laughed Kathy Casey. "They were Good Shepherd sisters, who ran a home for wayward girls years ago, so I guess they were used to wild girls—which I was. Mother Superior even made my prom dress—it plunged to my bellybutton and was slit up to my crotch. It was just gorgeous. Some of the older nuns with those giant habits would walk by while she was pinning my hem and say, 'Oh, oh, oh my, are you wearing a jacket with that, dear?'"

Kathy Casey is a force to be reckoned with. She describes herself as an "insane self-starter." Brassy, sassy and smart as a whip, she is fueled by passion: passion for good food and creative cocktails—from the simple to the exotic. Hailed by the late Craig Claiborne, food editor at the *New York Times,* as an "inventor of dishes that dazzle the eye and the palate," Kathy is a trendsetter. Early in her career, she was one of the youngest female executive chefs in the country. Kathy has been blazing pathways for women in professional kitchens since the mid-1980s.

"I grew up cooking and making things out of nothing. We didn't have a lot of money, so my mother and grandmother were always cooking up 'concoctions,' as they called them." Kathy left home at fifteen and landed a job cooking dinner for twelve nuns. "They took their meals very seriously, and dinner was the highlight of their day. I was on a budget, so I researched all these cookbooks, copied recipes and made up stuff. And then, while dinner was cooking, I'd go to the back pantry, smoke and do my homework. I used to cut their hair, too, and give them permanents, and pluck their eyebrows; I guess they were pretty progressive," she laughed.

Culinary school was her next objective, where she was thrown into the veritable frying pan. One of her instructors said to her, "Kathy, you'll never be a chef. You know, you should use your real talents—wink, wink." She looked at him and said, "'Screw you! I will be a chef and I'll be a famous chef. I'll bet you $500 right here and now.' He's dead, but he still owes me. Never tell me no. Oh, no. Never."

Kathy made a name for herself running one of the top restaurants in Seattle in the mid-1980s and helped to bring women chefs and Northwest cuisine to national prominence. "I beat some trails for women and, boy, was it crazy." Kathy definitely blazed some trails; she became executive chef at twenty-five-years old. "The management actually tried to make me wear a 'pantry dress' when I first started cooking! I told them if the guys put one on . . . I'd gladly comply," she said with spunk.

After Seattle, she did a stint in New York. "I loved to experiment, innovate with different tastes and find creative ways to present food. I created a triangle hamburger and bun and dressed it up with wild stuff—very edgy at the time. I was promptly fired. I should have known it wasn't a fit because, when I interviewed for the job, my boss had an eight-inch shag carpet that had to be raked."

After that kick in the pants, she started her own food and beverage consulting business called Kazzy & Associates while still in New York, then moved back to Seattle. In 1997 she purchased an 1889 brick building in Seattle's Ballard neighborhood, refurbished it with her husband John, and changed her company to Kathy Casey Food Studios: a food, beverage and concept consulting agency. And in 2002 she started Dish D'Lish cafes and specialty products.

"I am passionate about food. Have you ever gone to dinner and you're disappointed in the meal? I swear to God, it's because the person cooking is not loving what they're doing. You can taste love in food; you can taste the passion."

Twenty years later, Kathy is still a whirlwind of creativity and unconventionality. Passion, according to Kathy, is the catalyst of creativity. "If you're really passionate about something, your curiosity compels you to want to learn more; by learning more you try more things. If you have passion about what you're doing, you will always move forward. You want to be learning, you can't stop learning. You want to be creating; you want more. If you have passion, you always want more."

Kathy frequently challenges the current condition. After seeing the opportunity in specialty beverages and working with creative cocktail development, Kathy soon became a forerunner in the bar-chef scene. Thus, in 2002, Liquid Kitchen was established. "We're now one of the top cocktail-development companies nationally. And I love speaking about all the innovation and creativity we are seeing around spirits and the bar." The food world recognizes her ingrained disdain for the status quo. Greg Atkinson, *The Seattle Times' Pacific Northwest Magazine* columnist, recently wrote, "Kathy Casey, the iconoclast, has become the icon."

So where has this passion and creativity taken Kathy? Nine cookbooks, feature stories in numerous national publications, appearances on *Larry King Live, Good Morning America,* and the *Food Network*, her consulting agency's international expansion as well as Dish D'Lish cafés and specialty food line, to name a few places where she excels.

In the works are cocktail programs for international clients, a webisode cocktail series, and a reality television show as well as a full menu of other exciting projects. Kathy's passion is unending.

Following Her Bliss

Dayna Goldfine

Position: Filmmaker and Owner, Geller/Goldfine Productions & Storyline Productions | **Accomplishment:** Emmy Award winner, 1998; nominated by Directors Guild of America for Outstanding Directorial Achievement in the Documentary Form; film selected by Academy of Motion Picture Arts and Sciences as one of the outstanding documentaries of 1994 | **Birthplace:** Philadelphia, PA

Dayna Goldfine graduated from college hearing two cautionary tales. First, "you're a feminist studies major; you'll never get a job." Second, "even if you get a job but don't stay there for a year, no one will ever hire you again."

Dayna, as it turns out, did not heed her peers' "sage" advice back in 1982 and, instead, jumped from job to job: from a video post-production company, to a famous jewelry designer's workshop to a textbook publishing house, to assisting a pension consultant—all within twelve months. "The fact that I got hired after majoring in feminist studies made me kind of brave to keep changing jobs," she shook her head, laughing at herself.

Dayna has always followed her passion and interests. Even when the world told her differently, she has marched to her own drummer. "Doing what you are really passionate about, even when the world tells you that's not what you should do, has been my way. Being passionate about something means that you pick yourself up and keep going. It doesn't mean you won't trudge through a lot of mire along the way, but if your end in sight is something you are really in love with, the trudging gets easier."

Dayna's career path veered radically when she met her now-husband and business partner, Dan Geller. As he was completing his master's degree in documentary production, Dayna took a close look at Dan's passion and made a decision. "You know, I think I would really love to do this type of work. It's more intellectually and emotionally rewarding than dealing with retirement pensions all day," she said with a wink. In response, Dan encouraged Dayna to pursue her interest by enrolling in film school, so she could become "a partner and not his student," she explained.

"Art, creative writing, and drawing have always been avocations for me, and here was an opportunity to wed what I thought were pastimes into a full-scale focus," she added.

Now Emmy Award winners, director/producer Dayna Goldfine and husband Dan Geller have created critically acclaimed, multi-character documentary narratives that braid their characters' individual personal stories into a larger portrait of the human experience.

Serendipity has always played a large role in the film projects and none more so than with their first film, *ISADORA: Movement from the Soul*, in 1988—when Dayna was only twenty-seven. "I received a letter from a friend living in Paris who encouraged us to tell the Isadora Duncan story. Before we knew it, though we had not *yet* made the decision to do the film, we received a fateful letter from Paris. Madeleine Lytton, a third-generation Duncan dancer, had bought a plane ticket and would soon arrive expecting to be filmed."

At the time, Dayna was pretty unprepared to make the movie, but that didn't stop her, "You know, one thing about self-starters is they often say yes without having a clue as to how they're going to accomplish the yes!" she said. So Dan and Dayna scraped together a little money, didn't go on a honeymoon, asked their friends to donate time, quickly learned everything they could about Isadora Duncan, established connections with those in the dance world, and made the film happen.

After that herculean effort, "we vowed we would never make another dance documentary, especially a dead dancer," she laughed. In filmmaking, if you've had a success, everyone expects you to try to repeat it. So the question we were asked most often immediately after *ISADORA* was, "So what's your next dance documentary?" Dan and I had so many other subjects we wanted to tackle – why would we want to repeat ourselves? Unbeknownst to Dayna, that promise would one day be broken.

For Dayna, "Following my bliss means focusing fully and completely on what I love to do. In my world, that means choosing a subject to delve into that I am really passionate about, rather than deciding on a direction based on what gets funded." She believes that without "an incredibly deep and unsquashable passion," she could not have sustained all the negativity.

"As an artist you're discouraged from pursuing a path in general and from taking on a specific project in particular. Funders turn you down, family members push you towards other careers, distributors and directors reject you. But personal cheerleading and an absolute belief in the project energizes you."

In 2005, with several award-winning films under their collective belt, they once again took on the dance world with *BALLETS RUSSES*, a film that narrates the beginning days of a dance troupe that started with Russian refugees who collaborated with American, European and South American dancers and then ended up dazzling the world and revolutionizing the look of ballet in the first half of the twentieth century. "Funding documentaries on the arts is very difficult because those who fund them are looking for a film about political or social problems," she said solemnly.

In the winter of 2000, with an important proposal for *BALLETS RUSSES* in to a funding organization, Dayna received an important phone call. The representative from the organization said, "Well, we think your idea is boring. It's not relevant. We just don't see any merit. And in fact, we really would advise you not to proceed with this project."

Dayna hung up the phone, more determined than ever to do this film. "I think moments like this for self-starters galvanize—rather than discourage—your belief and your passion for what you want to accomplish. You just can't be afraid to go to the top." The outcome earned them numerous awards for *BALLETS RUSSES* including a selection to the "Top 5 Documentaries 2005," by the National Board of Review, acceptance into prestigious festivals such as Sundance and Toronto, and recognition on a dozen critics' Best Films of 2005 lists. *BALLETS RUSSES* also went on to screen theatrically and on television worldwide.

In the film world, critics abound. "I have learned to deal with the rude and bruising comments that can tear you down. If you let them affect what you decide to do or what you've accomplished, you really can't be a self-starter. Not that I don't have regular bouts of self-doubt and times when I lick my psychological wounds, but my belief in the value of my work sustains me." She added, "I just keep following my passion with determination and it always seems to work out."

Passionate About Others' Passions

Rob Ukropina

Position: Partner, Black Diamond Ventures | **Accomplishment:** California Small Business Person of the Year, 2007; founded Overnite Express | **Birthplace:** San Marino, CA

R ob Ukropina is a self-starter *par excellence*. He loves to start businesses and is passionate about helping others find their passion and develop it into a business.

He got his first lesson in business in 1963 when he was ten years old and growing up in San Marino. "My friend had an avocado tree. Our plan was to cut off the avocados, pull a wagon, and sell them at three for a quarter. I did all the pitches and he followed me with the wagon. At the end of the day, we split our take. I said, 'Okay we have $20; you get $10 and I get $10.' He said, 'No. I get $15; you get $5.' I asked, 'Why?' He said, 'Because I own the avocado tree.'"

This lesson, though a hard one to learn, stayed with Rob throughout his career and still resonates with him today. He reflected, "I get great joy out of helping others, but I guess the lesson learned is that some people do not want or appreciate the help. I approach each situation and person with an open heart—I'm here to help. Some take me up on it; others don't." But Rob had to experience some rocky times before he found his passion.

After college he took what he thought was the correct path for a recent graduate. "I went to work for corporate America so I could gain as much experience as possible. I thought you were supposed to work for a big corporation, learn everything you can and then eventually go out on your own," he said.

A sales job with a financial printing company gave him what he needed, which was income, a million-dollar, six-year contract and real-world experience.

In 1991, Rob was ready to launch his own business. "I left to become an entrepreneur at age thirty-six. It had been my dream to go out on my own—after all, I'm a third-generation entrepreneur—both grandfathers, and my dad," he added proudly. The idea of a leasing company appealed to him—helping companies get the equipment they needed for their businesses. "I had a partner who I thought was an entrepreneur too." Instead, the business folded. "We lost it all. My family and I went from living at the top of the hill to an apartment at the bottom, with three kids under eight years old," he said solemnly.

One year later, in 1992, Rob started Overnite Express from scratch. His concept was based on the FedEx and UPS delivery model, which was deliver packages overnight and on time. But his idea had an advantage because Overnite Express would pick up packages after the other two companies stopped.

"Entrepreneurs don't stop working at 5:00 p.m. when the big boys and girls go home. That's when FedEx and UPS end their day. That was our niche—we picked up until 9:00 at night," he said.

And that's where Rob found his passion by helping entrepreneurs become successful. Overnite Express fed his passion by delivering packages along with excellent customer service. His business practices reflect Rob's belief in people. "If you treat your associates well, your associates will treat your customers well, then your company becomes profitable. It becomes a circle of success."

Rob claims that this time around, he did the opposite of everything he had learned in corporate America. "I built Overnite Express based on the principles, or lack thereof, I learned in corporate life, such as listening, having humility and surrounding yourself with people who are smarter than you. Plus, I think passion is everything. Those who can figure out their passion early tend to be more successful. I think if you are living your passion you are having more fun. I was definitely having a lot of fun!" Rob said.

His desire to help people succeed—to nurture their passion—was incorporated within his company. "I did what was best for my employees. It's all about the people, all about servant-leadership; I encourage them along the way. I even negotiated a employment contract for a sales person who was leaving my company. I always had their best interest at heart," he said earnestly.

In 2008, after sixteen years leading Overnite Express, Rob was ready for another challenge. "I had done all I needed to do with this company. I loved working with my three hundred associates, but I was ready to move on. I was ready to work full-time helping other entrepreneurs start their businesses."

He sold his ownership in Overnite Express and joined Black Diamond Ventures, a venture capitalist business based in Glendale, California.

For Rob, the goal is the same, he said, "I'm thrilled to have guided hundreds and hundreds of people. Using my network to help people achieve financial success feeds me. I'm having a total blast mentoring entrepreneurs. These self-starters have a passion for an idea or service or product. They just need help getting to that destination."

KEYNOTES

Self-starters have passion for their life and their work. What they have chosen as their life's purpose imbues them with enthusiasm. It gets them up in the morning and sustains them throughout the day. It also provides them with a monetary reward for their effort.

Their passion (some might say it's more of an obsession), along with discipline, gives them energy to move forward even when life hands them curveballs.

Many people I meet through my workshops and speeches do not have passion; they look, as one of the self-starters stated, like the walking dead. They go through the paces of their work life and collect a paycheck. That's not for you! Your life will be much more fulfilling, purposeful and joyful if you are doing what you love.

Think about these questions:

1. What really gets me excited during my spare time? What activity do I engage in where time just slips away?

2. What really gets me excited at work? Is it a project? Working with a team? Working alone? Solving problems?

3. What do I do easily, naturally, in the flow? Or, what part of work is very natural and enjoyable for me (e.g., being creative, involved with people, analyzing facts or getting things done)?

4. If I could design the perfect career, what would that look like? Where would I be? What would I be doing?

Activities:

- Ask a dozen people who know you well: What are my greatest strengths? The common themes you hear will direct you towards your passion.

- Notice throughout your workday when you feel like you're working in the "zone" of satisfaction. It could be one thing or several things. Keep track as you notice those times. This activity can reveal your passion.

Four

Seizing Opportunity Capitalizes on Chance

Opportunity: Chance; occasion; random; opening; turning point; crucial period; timely.

Though some self-starters believe their success contains an element of "luck," in every instance they saw an occasion to realize their dream, move their vision forward or solve a complex problem. Their ability to see what others did not is a skill we can all learn.

The Art of the Possible

Gale Bensussen

Position: Operating Advisor/CEO, Coral Street Partners | **Accomplishment:** Grew company to become largest supplier in the U.S. of store brand nutritional supplements and over-the-counter drugs, selling more than 35 billion dosages a year; co-founded lab to find cause and preventive measures for Alzheimer's disease | **Birthplace:** Los Angeles, CA

Trouble was brewing.

The management team of a publicly held vitamin and nutritional products company had just received the bad news: their largest shareholder had decided to sell its controlling interest. The team was depressed; it felt like their company was being sold out from under them. These savvy intrapreneurs had bought the company years ago from its overseas parent company; they'd poured their heart and soul into growing it and then took it public.

Suddenly, the future looked bleak: no more management jobs, no more running the show and, even worse, they would have to go back to being regular employees after years of working and thinking like entrepreneurs.

As they bemoaned their fate around the conference room table that dark day in 1991, Gale Bensussen, senior vice president of marketing at the time, spoke up. "Let's do our own deal. Let's buy the company!"

Talk about seizing an opportunity, he reflected almost twenty years later. "That day, I looked at everyone sitting there and said, 'I can do it; I *will* do it. Why don't we take the risk?'"

They responded with, "You don't have any idea what you're doing. You've never done it before . . . but, okay, it's better than the alternative, which was doing nothing!"

With that support, and some coaching by the CEO, Gale headed to New York, slides in hand, to meet with the largest shareholder. "We closed a deal in 90 days and then took the company private," says Gale. And everyone breathed a huge sigh of relief.

Upon reflection, "it actually never occurred to me that we weren't actually qualified to do this," Gale said modestly. "It's just that I see things differently. I saw something the others didn't see. They didn't feel they were qualified; they didn't know how to raise the money to purchase the company. My response was that it just never struck me as an obstacle."

Gale sees self-starters as those who see opportunities others don't and who take responsibility to follow through on that opportunity all the way to closure. "So few people seize opportunities by embracing the problem, the situation, or the idea and then doing something to move themselves forward.

Most people won't risk failure. They just don't step up if there is a risk. "Those who do are flying in rarefied air," says Gale.

It's ironic an innovator like Gale would stay with the same company for more than thirty years but that's just what he did. Each new opportunity—and there were plenty of them—meant he could push the envelope again. He was the catalyst to build a pharmaceutical plant in China and establish an integrated venture in India for converting prescription pharmaceuticals to over-the-counter status.

"Generic drug companies don't do store brand over-the-counter products. But we saw an opportunity to partner with these companies; we could package, distribute and manufacture these products for them,"

Gale said thoughtfully. Thus, in 2001 (ten years after the employees bought back "their" company) they also grew their company to become the premier supplier of store-brand nutritional supplements and over-the-counter drugs to retailers around the world, selling over 35 billion dosages per year.

Once Gale sees an opportunity, his creative juices start flowing. "Opportunities are not so much about thinking *outside* the box, but simply trying to never get *in* the box in the first place. I call it the 'Art of the Possible.'"

For example, when nutrition product sales were slumping in 1993, he suggested creating a Body Shop-type approach for major drugstore chains: a group of products would be bundled and sold as a package. The reaction? "'Oh, we don't know how to do that. We can't do that.'"

Gale did it in anyway. The marketing team, with Gale's lead, made it happen and further proved Gale's theory on the Art of the Possible: the company's new, bundled product became the "Item of the Year" in the drug and mass merchandise trade—and created millions of dollars in sales.

For Gale, it's always been about moving ahead and plowing new ground; he's still doing it today. Using two ends of the generational spectrum—the Baby Boomers and the college set—Gale sees an opportunity to repeat earlier, similar successes to manufacture nutritional supplements in liquid form. "We're putting the product in college bookstores as well as on the Internet."

Another way he is contributing his expertise and resources is by funding—jointly, with his wife Jane—the Translational Laboratories at the University of Southern California in Los Angeles. They are focused on finding the cause and a preventive measure for Alzheimer's disease. They have already received several National Institute of Health grants for clinical studies. "We can do this!" Gale said passionately.

Two things we do know: There will be a noticeable lack of "boxes" to avoid getting stuck in. And the Art of the Possible is alive and well.

A *Real Housewife* Who Is Really Extraordinary

Vicki Gunvalson

Position: Founder/CEO, Coto Insurance & Financial Services, Inc.; cast member of NBC TV's *The Real Housewives of Orange County* | **Accomplishment:** Author; Founder of Coto University | **Birthplace:** Chicago, IL

It's hard to decide what is the most interesting facet of Vicki Gunvalson's life. Her role as one of the cast members on the reality television show, *The Real Housewives of Orange County*? Or the fact that she has built one of the most successful woman-owned insurance agencies in the United States?

The answer is both, and their common thread is her ability to seize opportunities.

"When I speak at women's groups, I tell them, 'Don't let the grass grow underneath you by waiting for someone to control your destiny. Keep doing what you do well, and doing it smarter, doing it better and more passionately than anyone else. It's up to you to seize opportunities that will take you where you want to go!'" Vicki's diligence, coupled with incredible energy, keeps her focused on her goal of financial security.

Her early work history hinted at future successes. She landed her first job at an ice cream shop. "I was the fastest ice cream scooper there," she giggled. Later, she worked in fast food and then ended up at a grocery store. "I became the fastest checker and got my name on the board every week for my speed!"

Vicki chose not to go to college; instead, she went to beauty school. After 1,500 training hours, she became a hair stylist—only to quit one month later.

"I was soul searching. College hadn't appealed to me; a career in hairstyling didn't either, as it turned out. So, I thought, 'Well, let's get married.' I married the guy I was dating because he owned a fast car and had a nice butt. It was a nightmare marriage. The only good to come out of it was my two amazing children." At age twenty-nine, Vicki was single, with two children, no education and no child support.

But opportunity struck one day as she purchased a life insurance policy. She casually asked the agent, "'How much did you make selling me this policy?' The agent answered, '$600.' I said, '*You* wrote a piece of paper and made $600?!'"

Four months later, insurance license in hand, Vicki sold a half-million-dollar life insurance policy to a thirty-two-year-old man. Unfortunately, he died within months, leaving a wife and three children behind. "I remember like it was yesterday, yet it was nineteen years ago. I arrived at the widow's home and I can picture her exactly—even what she was wearing. And I can still see her face. People were streaming in with cakes, casseroles and flowers. I came in with a $500,000 death check and said, 'You're gonna be fine. Your kids are gonna be fine and you can keep your house.' I literally changed that women's life and mine too. I knew this was my calling."

Vicki's diligence and keen ability to scan for opportunities was sharpened by two tragic lessons. First, her father's very successful business was destroyed when his secretary embezzled money by writing checks to fictitious employees. As if that weren't enough to deal with, he ended up with Alzheimer's—and no insurance—at age fifty-nine. "As

I helped pay for his care, I realized I could help others provide security so this situation would never happen to other people," she said.

As a result, in 1990 she founded Coto Insurance & Financial Services, which is a life, health and annuity insurance agency. "I am a very impatient person," Vicki freely admitted. "I look at people who say, 'Well, one day, I am gonna have some divine intervention.' But that doesn't work, because you have to look for the opportunities; you can't wait for someone or something else!"

In 2009, Vicki founded another company, Coto University, which she uses to train her insurance agents; she wants to teach them how to be successful so they—and their clients—never have to experience the tragedy she lived through. "Watching my father's health decline and dealing with his lack of insurance, and my struggle to pay for better care for him—that's something I don't want others to have to experience! I see how my business literally changes people's lives, and that's what keeps me going every day."

With 700 agents under her tutelage, Vicki has become an extremely successful businesswoman.

That success has led her to fame, or at least notoriety. In 2004, she became one of the original cast members of the reality television program, *The Real Housewives of Orange County*. Her son Michael wrote to the show's creator, Scott Dunlop, who had posted a small ad in their local community paper; he was looking for college students who were willing to appear on a reality television show. Instead, Michael wrote about his mother, who worked in her business full-time behind the privileged gates of Coto de Caza in southern California. The letter piqued Scott's interest because, a few months later, he arrived on her doorstep to interview her for his show.

Again, she saw an opportunity and seized it. "It's great," she said. "I can have fun with the show and also showcase my business." The 2010 to 2011 season marks the show's sixth year.

Vicki believes life is like a stoplight. "You stop. You go. But you don't stop and wait forever, you know. Don't wait for anybody else to get you what you want. Do it yourself. Control your own destiny. See where there's need and go for it—that's the definition of a self-starter!"

WHEN OPPORTUNITY KNOCKS, WING ANSWERS

WING LAM

Position: Founder/Co-Owner, Wahoo's Fish Taco restaurants | **Accomplishment:** Owns 56 restaurants throughout western United States | **Birthplace:** Sao Paolo, Brazil

How does a Chinese man who grew up in Brazil end up starting a Mexican restaurant chain in America? Because Wing Lam, co-owner with his two brothers and founder of Wahoo's Fish Taco restaurants, seized every opportunity presented to him and made lemonade out of lemons.

Wing has always been around the restaurant business—in fact, he literally grew up inside his parent's restaurant. "Our house was attached to it. To get to our living area you had to go through the restaurant.

"My parents were poor farmers and literally smuggled themselves out of China. They arrived in Sao Paolo, Brazil, in 1955 and started the first Chinese restaurants in Brazil. Thus, my life in restaurants began."

When he was fourteen, Wing and his family arrived in America. A few years later, in 1975, his parents duplicated their earlier success in Brazil by opening restaurants in southern California. Wing and his brothers also reprised their roles as general errand boys in the restaurant. "Anything that had to be done, we did. From peeling onions to washing dishes to waiting tables to mopping the floors—we did it all."

Once Wing started at San Diego State College, he seized the opportunity to work in the registrar's office. "That way, you get the classes you want, at the times you want, in the quarters you want," he recalled. After trying other programs at the university, Wing realized he wanted to join the business school. Once he was accepted to the program, he volunteered to give tours to incoming business students. Wing saw this as a chance to think through his own direction as he advised the students on possible areas of emphasis.

In his senior year, Wing realized that if he worked at the business school's internship office, rather than at an internship with one company, he could learn about all different types of businesses and narrow down his area of interest. That opportunity assisted him immensely, and he landed a job writing proposals for Sparta, Inc., a think tank for President Reagan's "Star Wars" program. When he was only twenty-five years old, his proposal won the contract that represented a quarter of all the company's business.

Despite such a huge success, Wing decided this was not the career path for him. He quit and took a job with a real estate franchise.

Once again, Wing saw opportunity where others may have overlooked it. As he looked through the listings of businesses for sale, he found "an old Italian joint for sale." Wing realized, "Oh, my God, that's a gold mine. It had seats for about eighty people, a full kitchen and a pretty good location." He borrowed money from his parents, enlisted the help of his two brothers and opened a "funky little taco place that people thought was weird as hell, since Asian guys ran it."

Then things got interesting.

Because the restaurant was ideally located close to the two top surfing apparel and product companies in the world, employees from both organizations started frequenting the place. Word of mouth created the buzz Wahoo's Fish Taco needed, and the next thing Wing knew, his staff received free uniforms (T-shirts from Billabong) and free shoes (from Quicksilver) for promotional purposes. "So, now, the No. 1 and No. 2 surf brands in the universe were giving us free stuff!"

When Billabong asked Wing to cater an event for the largest trade show in the action sports retail industry, he said yes. "Though I had never catered in my life, it was an amazing opportunity!"

Wing said, "In the surf culture, it's all about the stickers. So the companies were giving away free stuff, and I was getting free decorations for my restaurant! And today, our signature trademark is still stickers in our windows."

Then things really picked up steam. "All of sudden, through the network I'd built, people started calling for more catering gigs." Wahoo's Fish Tacos was officially launched, and word was out.

After the initial success of the first restaurant, it took ten years to add thirteen locations and then ten more years to get to a grand total of fifty-six.

Though the restaurant chain was successful, Wing never passed up an opportunity to expand. "We realized surfers were taking up snowboarding, and we saw another opportunity. So we opened Wahoo's in Colorado and California. Then, of course, we went to Hawaii because you go to Hawaii to surf. Then, on to Austin, Texas. We are now basically the official restaurant of the surf sport industry."

What's next for Wing? "Our newest opportunity is college campuses."

Wing credits his amazing success to his refusal to ignore an opportunity. "I believe there are two kinds of people in the world: those who can live knowing there may or may not be a paycheck on Friday, and those who can't. I'm the former. And I guess it helps that I see opportunity and go for it."

A True Leader, From Locker Room to War Room

Jeffrey Kendall Sapp

Position: Founder/President, J. K. Sapp Enterprises |
Accomplishment: Commanding officer of six warships; three master's degrees; first black co-captain of Naval Academy's football team; first black in Midshipmen history to be named All-American by NCAA Football's Division I | **Birthplace:** CO

According to Jeffrey Sapp, self-starters are those who think "what if?" rather than "as is," and who think "why not?" as opposed to "it's just not done!"

No one has walked his talk more profoundly than Jeffrey. His academic degrees, athletic honors and successes in a variety of high-profile leadership positions exemplify his belief that constantly asking those questions, listening to the answers and then taking appropriate action makes it possible to seize opportunities and achieve nearly anything.

Jeffrey's impressive successes were not written in the stars. An average student in high school, he turned to sports as a way to excel. He was considered too small to play Division I football, so he focused on his goal of trying out for the Olympic wrestling team. That work paid off—he received sixty scholarship offers at high school graduation.

Jeffrey thinks his race played a big part in the support he received for his athleticism. "For a young black man, being an athlete was one of those jobs that people encouraged you to pursue. They certainly weren't saying to me, 'Hey, go work on your PhD . . . although I did ultimately earn three master's degrees," he laughed.

Instead, he bucked the stereotype when he was accepted at the United States Naval Academy in 1973.

"My father pushed me towards the Academy. He saw it as a way to open doors for me as an officer, something he did not get to experience during his military service because, for the most part, racial segregation policies prohibited blacks from serving in leadership roles," Jeffrey said. Nonetheless, Jeffrey intended to play ball for the Navy. He said to himself, "'Why not?' I didn't wait for people to invite me. I just said, 'I'm gonna play football!'"

And, against all odds, at 5'11" and 197 pounds—a relatively small size for which few positions were open—he walked on to the Naval Academy's Division I team in 1973, with a schedule that year that was one of the toughest around.

This was exactly the opportunity he'd hoped to create, so he grabbed it—and ran with it, literally. Soon, sportswriters touted him as one of the best defensive nose guards in the nation. He went on to earn an impressive array of honors, including induction into the Navy Athletic Hall of Fame and being featured in an ABC Sports television special and other productions by CBS and NFL Films.

Most importantly, Sapp broke the color barrier when he was named co-captain of his team—the first black in the 165-year history of the U.S. Naval Academy.

"I had to do something that hadn't been done before, but I thought, 'Why not?' Still, attending this predominantly white university and being the runt on a big, giant football team was unfamiliar territory to me. I had to figure out how to do it. I knew if I wasn't comfortable outside my zone, I wouldn't survive," Jeffrey recalled, and explained what he figured out. "If you expand your comfort zone, it just gets wider and wider. The more folks and experiences that fall into it, the more stuff you learn, the more ideas you gather the more people you meet and the more opportunities present themselves."

Despite his accolades, on the one hand, and the tragedy of his parents' deaths after, on the other hand, he remained centered and focused. Jeffrey attributes this to his parents' earlier advice about taking advantage of opportunities and becoming the leader of the crowd, not one of the crowd.

After his graduation in 1977, Jeffrey saw more opportunities and he went for them. He earned a master's degree, commanded five different mine sweepers and then decided to attend the Naval War College. "I got in my head that I wanted to be captain so I started asking around, how would one get an early command? I found that, to be competitive, I should get another degree. I knew that when you initiate a process towards success, opportunities come your way. So I went back to school."

But Jeffrey didn't stop there. While pursuing his second degree, he also received his third master's degree at Salve Regina University. "I said to myself, 'Why not?' It sounded like a win-win for me. It would make me a triple threat and I would be prepared for any possibilities that came my way." That preparation would come in handy, as the sixth ship he commanded was an $800 million destroyer.

After his last command, he held a series of high-profile positions ashore, including several with such branches of the government as the Joint Chiefs of Staff, Bureau of Navy Personnel, Navy's Sea Systems Command and, later, the Navy League. Jeffrey viewed every assignment, he said, as one that would offer him opportunities.

Dr. Robert Schneller, Jr., author of the book *Blue & Gold and Black,* described Jeffrey, "Not only is Captain Sapp a role model for leadership and diversity, he is the architect for greater racial diversity among the Navy's civilian workforce and officer corps."

Sapp is also valued for his teaching, training and motivational skills. He's taught leadership to various U.S. government employees participating in leadership programs, served on two university campuses, worked as an international consultant on organizational strategy, and is, today, a sought-after speaker.

Opportunities—recognizing them, creating them, seizing them—are a common theme in the other area he's focusing on now, which is advising academic institutions, corporations, government agencies and military services on strategies for increasing the number of American students who study and pursue careers in science, technology, engineering and mathematics.

Jeffrey is thrilled and proud to fill his self-appointed role to "help young people, particularly young people of color, seek out and seize opportunities, because doing so is one of the keys to success and to achieving their dreams."

He firmly believes that if he hadn't grasped opportunities that came his way, he would never have fulfilled his own dreams. "Take every opportunity you can find," Jeffrey advises everyone from CEOs to students, "because you never know what could come of it."

KeyNotes

Self-starters grab hold of opportunities. They walk—not with abandon but with purposeful thought—through that partially opened door and see what's on the other side.

I have a sticky note next to my computer monitor. The note says: *What opportunity could this be?* It reminds me to consider every encounter as an opportunity for growth, learning or business development.

Questions to answer:

1. Do you easily notice potential opportunities?

2. Have you ever had an experience you thought was going to have a negative outcome and instead turned out to be an amazing opportunity?

3. What are current opportunities for you at work or in life? If you can't list any, what could you do to create some? Volunteer on a project? Go back to school for more training? Hire a life or career coach?

Activities:

- Create a method for looking at potential opportunities. Make it be a part of every consideration, even if you're a bottom-line person. For example, turn that idea—that project—on its head: see if any other approaches come to mind rather than the straight-line solution.

- Write about a time when you passed up an opportunity, only to later wish you had grabbed it? What was that like for you?

FIVE

SELF-MOTIVATION DRIVES PROGRESS

S elf-Motivation: Self-determination; inspiration; impetus; driving force; impulse; stimulus; incentive; inner motivation.

The get-up-and-go to get up and get going illustrates this trait. These people could be characterized as driven, passionate and spurred on by an internal energy to move ahead. Awards, rewards and incentives do not motivate them as much as the desire to achieve their goals.

Cutting a Wide Swath of Experience

Jim Ellis

Position: Dean, Marshall School of Business, University of Southern California (USC) | **Accomplishments:** Founding Director of Professional Business Bank; Director of the Fixed Income Funds of The Capital Group; established USC-China Institute | **Birthplace:** WA

Jim Ellis, dean of Marshall School of Business at University of Southern California (USC), fits into all three self-starter categories—intrapreneur, entrepreneur and academician. He worked his way up the corporate ladder within several companies, owned multiple businesses and now fulfills a key role at USC, where he is responsible for the education of 5,700 students, both graduate and undergraduate. His banker father advised Jim during college that it was important he understand numbers and how to use them to better guarantee his future success in business, no matter which specific industry he worked in.

Jim was all ears. To get a good understanding of accounting and finances, Jim worked in the Sears, Roebuck and Company's credit department. "I really learned about credit reports and personal credit," says Jim. But his real-life learning came when he was a bill collector. "I actually collected in two of the most difficult parts of the country—Indian reservations in New Mexico and south central Los Angeles. I learned a lot about myself, such as about being motivated to get up early on a Saturday morning and trying to coerce money out of people. Those were tough experiences." Tough they may have been, but those early lessons were crucial to Jim's later business success.

After graduating with an MBA from Harvard in 1970, Broadway Department Stores hired Jim. "Another piece of advice my father gave me was to be the first guy to work in the morning," he recalled. "In fact, so early that when the second guy comes in, the hood on your car is cold. You don't leave early; you stay until the work is done." With that inner drive, he received numerous promotions, which took him to the upper echelons in the company.

Having a strong work ethic is essential for a self-starter, according to Jim. "The more time you are working and thinking about your business, the more creative you can be on how to make the business even better."

Jim says that being a self-starter comes with a lot of hard work. "Self-starters are those who, when they hear the alarm clock, they jump out of bed and say, 'Oh, my God, I've got to get going!' They are just driven to start their day, as opposed to those who just pull the pillow over their head and say, 'You know, let's just sleep for another hour.'"

Because of the enormous amount of time Jim has spent at his office, opportunities appeared right and left. "I was invited to go out to dinner with visiting CEOs from other companies and, through those connections, exciting circumstances presented themselves."

He left the large retail chain in 1983, bought a business the same year and sold it a year later, and then went to work as CEO of American Porsche Design from 1985 through 1990. During that time, the company opened many new retail accounts, selling products complementary to the Porsche automobile; the first retail Porsche Design concept store was also opened during his leadership.

Still, those successes left Jim unsatisfied. "I went to the top of the corporate ladder and then decided I wanted to be my own boss. I wanted to be an entrepreneur again." For the next six years, starting in 1991, Ellis was involved with nine companies as owner, part-owner or partner, along with the roles of chairman and CEO for an upscale, highly acclaimed home accessory store in southern California.

His inner motivation to explore different businesses cut him a wide swath of experience and prepared him for his next career move.

Jim used to be a member of Young Presidents' Organization (YPO), which has a rule that members are not allowed to be in the group after they turn fifty. "At age forty-nine and a half, my pals asked me, 'So, what are you going to do next?' I said, 'What are you talking about? All I know how to do is run companies and build businesses!'"

They instructed him to get out a clean sheet of paper and, with no constraints, write down what would really motivate him. "I wasn't too keen on that little exercise, and I told them so.

"They said, 'You have thirty days, then come back and tell us. Your answers will help you plan the next twenty-five years.'" Thirty days later, he told the group, "With twenty-five years of experience, what really motivates me is to share my knowledge with others. That means I would teach, speak, write and consult."

A YPO member responded, "Well, go do it!"

Jim answered, "Well, I don't have a PhD so I can't teach. I can't write because I don't have a topic. I could consult but who's going to hire me? If I were going to do speeches, I'd need a really good shtick. But I really like this idea." The group told him to figure it out and report back in six months. His wife, when he told her about it, was tremendously supportive of the change as well.

Once he decided these four areas were his new direction, yet no paths had been revealed, he decided "to just keep my eyes open." Within two weeks, he received a phone call telling him of a position as a marketing professor at USC. Jim's response was, "But I don't have a PhD!"

"Oh, but you don't need one," the caller answered. "It's a teaching job."

"I came, interviewed and literally—within six months of writing down those four goals in 1997—I had realized them," said Jim, satisfied.

Since then, Jim has held the position as professor of marketing at USC, as well as dean since 2007. "I stepped off the cliff and said, 'Oh, wow, where am I going?' That could have been a long fall to the bottom of the canyon, but fortunately a parachute appeared and I floated down. It's been pretty cool," he smiled.

In 2003, Ellis was honored with both the *Teaching Has No Boundaries Award*, co-sponsored by USC's Center for Excellence in Teaching, and the *Golden Apple Award*, given by USC Marshall School students. In 2004, he received the USC Parents' Association's *Outstanding Teaching and Mentoring Award*.

As for the consulting and speaking, Jim has traveled nationally and internationally, speaking on such topics as leadership and family-owned businesses. He also serves on several corporate and non-profit boards. His inner motivation constantly drives him to do more, bigger and better things.

A LIFE WELL-PLAYED WITH PLENTY OF TIME ON THE CLOCK

PAT HADEN

Position: Athletic Director, University of Southern California |
Accomplishment: Rhodes Scholar; Academic All-American |
Birthplace: NY

"Live your life so that you have standing-room-only at your funeral." This wise adage from Pat Haden's mother speaks volumes as to how Pat has led his life.

Many monikers can be ascribed to Pat. Rhodes Scholar. Professional football player. Attorney. Businessman. Football color commentator for NBC Sports. Athletic director. All apply. Not surprisingly, Pat has always been a strongly motivated, goal-oriented individual.

Born in New York to working-class Irish parents, Pat was the fourth of five children. He was a paperboy for a number of years, then, at sixteen, a commissioned shoe salesman. He was successful enough that he actually led a sales team one summer. "It was pretty interesting, since everyone was at least twenty years older than I!" he laughed.

Pat also delivered flowers and even made bouquets. On one memorable day, a recipient rejected a bouquet he created. "Well, as a young person, and even though it was my first flower arrangement, that rejection kind of hurt my feelings. But I went back to the shop and made it right," said Pat. Though this incident is simplistic in its retelling, it exemplifies Pat's dogged determination to be successful—at whatever he did.

Pat will tell you that self-starters are determined, focused individuals. "To be successful, you must be inner-motivated. Life hands you lots of difficulties and setbacks. You just need to get past them. Self-starters have this burning desire to be successful at something and realize that they have complete control over their destiny. You just don't have to rely on other people for your success," he says with deep conviction.

Pat received much of this driving force from his mother. "You know, I was never the greatest athlete; I was never the greatest student but somehow or other, I learned about being inner-motivated from my mother. It was important to her that we excel in a variety of fields. She always wanted me to come in first place, whether I was selling Christmas cards or candy or competing in athletic events."

In high school, football practice was just an addendum to Pat's workout because he also put in long hours practicing throws to his receivers. His focus paid off, as he was highly recruited by colleges. "I think, when you first start out, it's because you really love it, you really enjoy it. Then you kind of get addicted to success and want more of it. One quarter at a time," he said.

At the University of Southern California (USC), he played varsity football at the quarterback position. While there, he made three Rose Bowl appearances and his team won two national championships. Pat was also honored as a two-time Academic All-American and graduated *magna cum laude* and Phi Beta Kappa from USC in 1975.

Pat wasn't finished with either his academic or athletic career. After one year playing for the World Football League, he attended Oxford University on a Rhodes Scholarship. From there he joined the Los Angeles Rams in 1976 while pursuing his next goal of becoming an attorney. During the off-season and at night, he attended law school.

"It took me four and a half years to get through," he said matter-of-factly. It seems like this parallel path was to be his future—academics and athletics.

During his years with the Rams, it was his drive to achieve his goals that propelled him forward—even though disappointment and several injuries sidelined him. His last stay at the hospital changed his career. "I was in a hospital bed. It was 1981 and I was recovering from knee surgery, about to be traded to the Denver Broncos, when my phone rang. This fellow from CBS wanted to know if I was interested in broadcasting college games. I thought to myself, 'This could be an interesting new goal—I'll give it a try.' And I've been at it for twenty-six years," he said. An ironic side note Pat will often cite is his work during the last several years as a broadcaster for Notre Dame football—a team he handily beat while at USC. "My mother really wanted me to go to Notre Dame, so my tribute to her is that I always light a candle in her memory at the Grotto whenever I am on campus."

Besides his weekend broadcasting, Pat joined a private equity firm, which allowed him to take his skill sets from his various career paths and apply them to helping entrepreneurs reach their goals and achieve their dreams. But Pat's biggest challenges lie with his 2010 position as athletic director for USC, which is a school with a strong athletic history that's been hit with numerous National Collegiate Athletic Association (NCAA) sanctions.

His goal is to carry on USC's strong tradition with fairly played games on a level playing field. "We want to be competitive and plan to be. One of my goals is to continue the excellence of the USC athletic program," Pat said.

"To be a self-starter, you have to be able to navigate and negotiate around the bumps in the road, the failures, without getting discouraged," said Pat. "Sometimes you have to be downright creative to figure out how to achieve your goals when things get tough."

He is being asked to once again set his sights towards the end zone and throw straight and true.

Answering The Big 'Why?' Question

Quy "Q" Nguyen

Position: Founder/CEO, Allyance Communications, Inc. |
Accomplishments: Founded a successful communications intermediary with sustained, double-digit growth rates; supports over 20 children's charities | **Birthplace:** Vietnam

Asking—and answering—The Big "Why?" Question, as he calls it, has ruled Quy Nguyen's life for as long as he can remember.

"As long as I keep in mind *why* I'm doing something, I stay on the right track," he explained. "If I'm exhausted and feel like I can't give any more, I think of *why* I am doing it. Revisiting the reasons helps me gain strength and be more motivated. I think The Big 'Why?' determines a person's success as a self-starter."

The Big "Why?" Question is part of Quy's ethos. It's how he makes daily decisions, big and small.

"I was very motivated at an early age to have a better life," he said. "My big 'Why?' answer back then, and even still today, was my mom. I've always had this mindset that I need to succeed so I could help my mom; it has been a theme in my head all the time. After watching her struggle for so many years—struggling to raise us, to teach us values and ethics, all while not knowing a lick of English—I was determined to help her as soon as I could," he said fervently. "I was motivated to make something of myself so that my mother could have a better life. She was the heart and soul of the family and my driving force."

At six years old, Quy was "dropped off," along with his brother and mother, into the projects of Hartford, Connecticut. "My dad sponsored us to come to the states from Vietnam. But he deserted us after six months with no support and no one to help us navigate the English language. It was a very bad environment—in fact, of my friends from elementary school, all but a few are either dead or in jail," he said sadly.

Life as a new immigrant was not easy. "We all worked—my mother seven days a week. There's the old joke about how your parents walked miles in the snow to take you to school or to go to the store—we actually lived it. Two miles each way to school; three miles each way to the store. A luxury meal for us was Kentucky Fried Chicken. We were surviving on one hundred dollars a week. We even had our house robbed, and there was nothing to steal!"

Quy quickly mastered the English language, but his smart mouth got him in trouble at school and into fights. Because the majority of the neighborhood's African-American students had not seen many Asians, the other kids were constantly goading him to "do his karate moves"—the ones they had seen on television. Quy knew none, but "I knew how to run fast!" he chuckled.

By junior high, Quy realized he had no future in Hartford. "I knew I had to get out. My teachers were making fun of my nationality, and I was still getting into trouble," he said with a slight choke. "I begged my father to let me live with him in California so I could escape and get a better education."

Quy's determination led him out of the projects. He defied the odds by finishing high school and continuing on to college. Quy desperately wanted to graduate college but had no means to pay for it. To help pay his tuition, he started two small businesses based on needs he saw around him. Many of his friends returned home during each school holiday, so he started a travel agency. He also started a small flower shop and created and sold chocolate roses during the holidays.

After college and amidst the dot-com frenzy, Quy and two friends started a company to help businesses raise capital. They sold it when the Internet bubble burst—by this time, Quy was twenty-seven years old. The acquisition didn't create the financial rewards he had hoped for nor was it enough to help him meet his goals. Determined to succeed in a bigger way, he soon started another company, Allyance Communications.

Now in its eighth year, Allyance operates as an intermediary for voice, data, bandwidth and hosting services, and counts such companies as Forever 21, Vonage, Lionsgate, and Zappos.com as clients.

With this success, Quy has been able to check off some of the goals he wrote on a 3" x 5" card years ago. First on his list was "help mom retire." Though she still works today, now it's for fun and to keep active. With a house completely paid off and no debts, she's financially stress-free and is able to travel the world with Quy's monetary support. Quy was also able to return to Vietnam to visit the family he had not seen since fleeing the country at the age of six. "There was no greater pleasure than to go back to Vietnam with my mom and be able to financially help our relatives! I felt like Santa Claus, handing out $100 bills to each relative and buying simple things, such as a bed, a bicycle and clothes, that we take for granted. Not only was the experience surreal and rewarding, but to witness everyone look up to my mom and see how she had raised her kids despite her circumstances—that was priceless!"

Quy has had an amazing journey, and used The Big "Why?" Question to guide his inner drive. "It makes you work on a Friday afternoon when everybody is leaving for the weekend. It motivates you to make one more phone call or go out and get one more business card. It pushes you on when you get one more rejection!" he said fervently. Today, he's motivated for a better life by his love for his wife and children, as well as his mother. "My 'Why?' is so strong, and that's why I work so hard."

Thanks to Quy's leadership, vision and entrepreneurial spirit, Allyance has steadily experienced double-digit growth year after year since he started it in 2002. Supporting the community is a core value to Quy and Allyance, so the company has supported at least twenty children's charities over the years. He has been an active volunteer for the past ten years at Camp Footprints, a camp in California for disabled kids. Quy also mandates that all of Allyance's vendors participate in or sponsor one of his many charities. "We focus on children-related charities because it's organizations like the Boys & Girls Club that helped me stay out of gangs as a youth. Children are our foundation and our future!"

A great American success story, Quy has dramatically improved his life and that of many others. And he's done so by directing his determination and self-motivation toward the answers he gets when he asks himself that ever-present question lurking in his mind, The Big "Why?" Question.

Enterprising from Day One

Patrick Pascal

Position: President, Chelsea Management Company |
Accomplishment: Author, *Kesling Modern Structures*; President of firm
with over $1 billion in managed assets | **Birthplace:** Ireland

Patrick Pascal has been driven from the get-go. At five years old, he ran lemonade stands before he knew how to make lemonade. At ten, he organized soapbox races—for a profit. At eleven, he ran a local newspaper—gathering news, printing the content, and selling copies in the neighborhood. Again, for a profit.

Despite his inner drive, some childhood enterprises didn't work so well. "I certainly learned what I didn't want to do. One was to not be a chicken farmer. When I figured out that my 220 chickens—even though I had a great little enterprise selling eggs—didn't know when it was Christmas or Easter or, in fact, any holiday . . . they just kept on going, even though I wanted a day off!" His worm business? Nope.

Scratch that. He also ruled out cattle ranching and working on assembly lines—two jobs he held during high school.

The seminal tutorial that bubbled up for Patrick occurred when he was twelve. His father gave him fifteen shares of $15-per-share stock. "I remember sitting on the arm of his chair at breakfast, looking through the stock tables in the newspaper. He loved explaining them to me; he even showed me how to read an annual report and P&L statement. He really gave me a huge gift, which was not only the opportunity to apply what I had learned but also the confidence, the belief in myself, that I could really do this," he reminisced. All through high school, Patrick played the market. With his earnings, he bought a car for high school graduation and had enough money to travel.

"You know, when I think about self-starters, I think about the fact that a lot of people go through life as if they're riding a raft down the river. Life goes by as they observe. Sometimes they roll to the right bank, sometimes to the left, or perhaps they catch an extra fish along the way. Self-starters are just the opposite. They aren't just along for the ride. They are motivated to determine *when* they want to go upstream or downstream or directly across the river," he said confidently.

Patrick did not follow the traditional college model of finishing school and then pursuing a career. Instead, he jumped right in when the lure of the stock market pulled him onto the exchange floor his sophomore year. He started as a runner, then became a clerk, and progressed to a specialist, a post he held for ten years. "When I was offered the specialist position, it was just too big of a job, too *good* of a job. It didn't seem logical to turn that down to finish college, when, at the time, the specialist pay was twice what the business school grads were making."

Needless to say, he took the job and did so well at it that in 1990, he formed his own investment company, Patrick Pascal Associates. In 1997, he was invited to join the investment committee at Chelsea Management Company, and, in 2002, he merged his own company into Chelsea Management, which manages investment portfolios for pensions, endowments, charities and wealthy individuals. In 2009, he was named president.

Motivated to complete what he had started, Patrick returned to the University of Southern California in 1996. "Having formed my own business, I went to the Marshall School of Business and told them what I had done with the full expectation that they would just bow down, give me a bunch of credits, hand me a diploma and call it good."

Their response? "Register and finish your degree."

His response? "I had the most amazing educational experience, even though it took me ten years of going part-time. I met fabulous professors, wrote a book and had the experience of a lifetime.

"To be a self-starter, I think you have to be motivated, but it also takes a large degree of self-confidence to push through the negativity and not be frightened by the prospect of failure. You say to yourself, 'I'm going to get there, come hell or high water. I am going to keep going, no matter what.'"

During his early years as a young specialist in the industry, Patrick was called into a partner's office and told he was in the wrong business; that he didn't have what it takes. "I wasn't rough or tough enough," Patrick grinned. "Well, self-starters love to prove people wrong. I mean, it only drives you harder! Every setback, every failure—from the lemonade stand to losing big trades on the exchange floor—prepared me for eventual success."

Patrick said that, while challenges can really defeat and discourage a person, "You just have to say to yourself, 'I'm going to keep going.' You must refuse to listen to the cynicism or be easily swayed by others. You have to call on your reserves and move forward." He believes in the value of failure. "Early success isn't always helpful early in your career. Failure is paying your tuition but outside the college walls."

What motivates Patrick is the art and science of managing money—the intersection of those two disciplines—and how it creates strategies that reward his clients as well as the firm. "Once you have the science of investing down pat, you have to apply the art—that's what energizes me. When I look at a nicely made portfolio, I get the same reaction as if I'm looking at a beautiful painting or sculpture. It's like, 'Wow, look at the balance, the color and the composition.' That's what gets me up in the morning!"

The idea of volunteering and contributing to the community is a driver for Patrick as well. "Every person has an obligation to leave the world a better place. If you don't do that, you lose your place in the world; you lose why you're here on earth. It's really important to not get yourself so tied up in what you're doing that you lose your perspective." To prove his point, Patrick volunteers at several charities that help the disadvantaged, and he sits on several boards of directors in the community.

Patrick believes that by achieving this balance—community service as a counterpoint to a capitalism-focused career, education vs. career, family vs. work, and the opposing yet symbiotic blend of art and science when building successful portfolios—he can more easily see problems and challenges from disparate perspectives and create solutions.

Perspective, balance, discovery—these are skills that drive Patrick's self-motivation and determination.

Kissing Frogs Leads to Great Success

Arlen "Arnie" I. Prentice

Position: Chairman, Kibble & Prentice | **Accomplishment:** Co-Founded $80-million-dollar financial services company; Philanthropist | **Birthplace:** WA

With his family on and off welfare and a father who drank too much, Arnie Prentice had a rough start. "It wasn't a very happy household," he said wryly. "There were many times that, with very little money, I had to bail my father out of jail. I often found him in places where he shouldn't be with people he shouldn't be with. Once I even coaxed a judge to get him out.

"Oh, and did I mention my great-grandmother was a madam and her 'ladies' used to babysit me?" he chuckled.

Arnie, a humble man with a gentle warmth about him, claimed he has spent his life trying to catch up. That may be true; if so, he more than met his target. Arnie and his partners have built one of the largest independent and privately held insurance and financial services business in the Pacific Northwest, now in its thirty-seventh year.

Arnie's personal story is one of grit, determination and the motivation to become someone. "You must define yourself rather than have others define you. You must take that inner motivation and determine your vision of where you want to go, who you want to be, what you want to do and what legacy you want to leave for the world. How you frame your answers will motivate you to succeed. That's the definition of a self-starter," he said.

Many of Arnie's experiences as a youth helped determine his path and motivate him to succeed. "On July fourth, the year I was sixteen, I had just spent the last eight hours on a tractor. I was tired, dirty and had been eating dust all day. I'd been watching the parade of people in convertibles or those who were towing their boats as they left for the holiday, and I got to thinking 'There's got to be a better way to live than what I'm doing!'"

Arnie had an even bigger glimpse of how the other half lived during the years he drove a school bus for a very upper-crust private school. "You can only imagine the homes I picked these kids up from. That was an experience."

Arnie's keen intelligence, work ethic and curiosity attracted adults who took him under their wing. "There was a collage of people, of mentors, throughout my life who really shaped who I am today." Some of the mentors taught him more sophisticated manners, such as how to order at a restaurant, how to dress, how to travel, how to check into a hotel, how to become more confident. "I learned what the rest of the world was like, and I knew I would never look back."

A real turning point for Arnie occurred in the early 1970s when he attended a workshop facilitated by Lou Tice of The Pacific Institute. "Lou talked about determining your own life; becoming inner-directed and motivating yourself to achieve great things. As a young man, I often whined about my family background, so I was pulled up sharp when Lou asked me, 'So, how old *are* you, anyway?' It took me about thirty seconds to get his point. That was the day I stopped letting my parents and my shortfalls determine the course of my life."

With that, Arnie started his career in financial services. He quickly made a name for himself and in 1972 started a business with partner Ted Kibble. "We were not going to be paralyzed by 'what ifs.' We just forged ahead," he recalled. "We were going to build our own business and let the chips fall where they may. Early in my career, a business colleague helped me understand that fear vanishes when imagination ceases and action begins. You have to take the first step. You have to get busy, and move forward. The very act of that beginning will motivate you."

Arnie is emphatic about not waiting for others' approval; you just have to ignore the naysayers, he said. "Ted and I knew we would have to kiss some frogs to get where we wanted to go, but that was okay."

Arnie's credo goes something like this: "You will confront unpleasant situations and unpleasant people in your life—everyone does. If you must kiss the frog, no matter how disagreeable, do not wait. Do not procrastinate; fight your way through it. Pull from your inner resources and motivate yourself. So many people avoid issues. Issues never go away, and they just become bigger and more problematic."

They may have kissed some frogs along the way, but by 2010, Kibble and Prentice had grown to offices in four cities, managing billions of dollars with over three hundred employees.

As chairman of Kibble & Prentice, Arnie has been giving back to the community for years. Not surprisingly, his goal is to help those who may have had a rough start in life. His company has been repeatedly recognized for its commitment to the community and its efforts to stamp out domestic violence. Between Arnie's personal efforts and those of his company, over two dozen charities have benefitted from over $40 million raised in support of the arts, education, and health. Additionally, Kibble and Prentice associates serve in civic organizations and on the boards of non-profit organizations, all in an effort to make volunteering a part of their responsibility as good citizens.

Wouldn't his mentors be so proud? But certainly not surprised at everything this self-motivated self-starter has accomplished.

Compelled to Work in No Man's Land

Mikala Rahn

Position: Director, Learning Works! Charter School | **Accomplishment:** Founder of school for probation youth, former dropouts and at-risk teens | **Birthplace:** CA

If ever there was a force of nature, it's Dr. Mikala Rahn. With a booming voice and a passion and work ethic that would make most of us pause, she has turned a failing experiment into an award-winning charter school.

"Thirty percent of the student body consists of youth on probation. That's why we located the school in no man's land. It works because there are no gangs in this territory," said Mikala of Learning Works! Charter School, located on the outskirts of Pasadena, California.

As the founder and school director, Mikala works with local dropouts. The school's student body consists of teenagers who have moved beyond the "at risk" designation to something worse. Some teens have served time in juvenile hall for serious crimes. Others have sunk into heavy drug use, and many female students have dropped out of school after they got pregnant.

In less than two years, Mikala and her team have touched the lives of 350 students. These students are the "bottom, bottom poorest kids" in Pasadena. "The families find us; they are so desperate for help," she said, adding, "It's a district embarrassment that there are so many dropouts."

For Mikala, being a self-starter is about intrinsic motivation. "It's something inside that makes you want to accomplish something. That inner motivation might have different purposes. For me, it's to save youth. But self-starters know there are no shortcuts, and to achieve anything takes a lot of hard work."

Mikala initially worked for Pasadena Unified School District in a dropout re-enrollment effort. She said it became too hard to tailor district practices to fit the needs of students who had dropped out, so she set out to create an independent school that could.

"And I love my work. Love it, love it! This is the whole of me. The desire to help these students be successful is the intrinsic motivation for me. I know that all youth are 100 percent redeemable, and I insist that a high school education is a right for every student," she said passionately.

Mikala saw firsthand what a life without a high school diploma is like: her mother never graduated, and suffered the consequences. "Maybe it's my family background that drives me forward. I never wanted to have my mother's life because she had no college education and a minimum wage job. She was poor when she was growing up; so was my father. Consequently, we were poor. It was really a very abusive home life with my alcoholic father. So, I decided my life was not going to be like that."

And Mikala is hell-bent on helping young people avoid that life as well. She targeted the toughest kids to work with: those disenfranchised by the school system and disengaged from education. "The school doesn't exactly recruit students for our program. Dropouts know dropouts, so they find us," she said. The school then deploys "chasers"—adults not much older than the students themselves, who accompany students as they overcome such hurdles as daunting doctor visits or court appearances. The chasers also deliver homework and urge students to come to class.

Mikala's credentials came to her the old-fashioned way—she worked hard, starting when she was very young. At age eleven she was vacuuming houses, and at fourteen she started a swim-lesson business. "I was saving money to get the hell out of there!" she said.

Mikala never took it easy, not even in college. She worked full-time while diving into a packed course load that explored the concepts of teaching and learning; specifically, where the two intersect in the brain. This passion led to two master's degrees and a PhD, which led to consulting work in socioeconomics and racial inequities, which led to starting a tutoring program for at-risk students, which, at last, led to starting the charter school.

Though Mikala loves the charter school and believes in its important work, the experiment has definitely had its drawbacks. "It's not just the personal financial hardship that will be hard to recover from, or the physical toll that this work has taken on me, or the sometimes overwhelming odds these kids face—it's just that I have to do this. It's the drive in my life. It's something inside of me that I must accomplish. I am mission-driven, which is extremely fulfilling and extremely exhausting. But I have God by my side. I couldn't have done this without a lot of prayer and miracles," she said passionately. "Since I started the charter school, I have gone from just some goodnight prayers to a God-centered existence."

Mikala believes everyone has the potential to be a self-starter, but not everyone has the intense motivation she does. "I am surrounded by self-starters. But the fact is, they quit. They give up too soon. I am astounded how many humans just give up when the going gets tough. They simply throw in the towel."

Not Mikala. She just uses the towel to wipe her brow as she moves forward.

RELATIONSHIP GURU AND SEX EXPERT

PEPPER SCHWARTZ

Position: Professor of Sociology, University of Washington |
Accomplishment: Author of sixteen books and fifty scholarly articles;
Recipient of American Sociological Award for the Public Dissemination of
Information | **Birthplace:** Chicago, IL

Pepper Schwartz, PhD, has always had an open attitude towards discussing sex. "In 1956, I was eleven years old and my mother told me she had a little sex education book for me. If I wanted to read it, she said, I could find it in the linen closet. I guess that's why today I get aroused by warm towels," chuckled Dr. Pepper Schwartz, a relationship guru and sex expert based in Seattle.

That book, along with an incident with her best friend, soon led Pepper and her mother to start a sex education discussion group. "My friend ran crying—sobbing—to me, certain she was evil and going straight to hell. I pulled out the little book and showed her that her sexual feelings were normal. She immediately felt better. So I went into the kitchen and said to my mother, 'I've saved Mary and we can save others.'"

With seven of Pepper's friends and their mothers, they started a group that met "in our knotty-pine-paneled basement," Pepper laughed. She also started a newsletter, which she sold for five cents, as a companion to the meetings. "That's when my entrepreneurial self-starting talent first displayed itself. Unfortunately, the group just petered out after a year and a half."

Coming from an active, multi-faceted, high school experience, Pepper hit Washington University in Saint Louis, Missouri, with energy and enthusiasm. "I did it all: cheerleader, sorority president, and I graduated magna cum laude in sociology." But it was at Yale, as she did her master's and doctoral work in sociology, that her focus solidified into a lifelong interest in sexuality and relationships.

Pepper believes self-starters are "self-starters because they have something driving them internally. They really have to follow their own path. They are not namby-pamby. They are willing to figure out how to get there because they just *have* to. It doesn't mean you have all the tools, but you go and figure out who does.

"At Yale there was this standard: not how many books you have read, but how many books you have written. It was very clear what it took to be somebody worth talking to." So Pepper wrote a book: *The Women of Yale* with Janet Lever. The publication's notoriety landed them on the *Today Show* in 1971. That was Pepper's first national television show, and it cemented her belief that she was on the right path.

Then, for research purposes, she took a job as a discussion leader for sessions following a sex education class for Yale undergrads. "I originally thought it would just be interesting research, but I was captivated with the politics of sexuality and the gender differences between men's and women's rights. The oppressiveness of family gender roles as they existed at the time fascinated me." That work led her, at age twenty-three, to co-write a pamphlet titled, *How to Have Sex without Getting Screwed*.

As Pepper finished graduate school in the late 1970s, a national conversation raged about women and their role in society. Once she obtained her doctorate, she was eager to secure a university position.

The University of Washington in Seattle hired her without an interview. "I call that luck," laughed Pepper. "Granted, I had a book and some articles, but the timing was perfect."

Because of the general interest in her topic, Pepper began doing television interviews, writing magazine articles and lecturing internationally. By reaching out to the public, Pepper found her life's work. "I realized that once you break norms and question them, you create your own pathway and that changes you," she said.

Though Pepper loved the media work, she knew she needed quantitative data for her subject to be professionally valuable within the academic community. Over the last three decades, she has gathered data, researched and wrote sixteen books and many scholarly articles and continued her mission to improve the lives of adults by enhancing their relationships. She offers counsel on everything from sex and health issues to communication within a relationship. "As a self-starter, I was driven internally to accomplish something because I just had to. I couldn't help myself!"

In 2003, Pepper created an intake test for an Internet dating service, Perfectmatch.com to help those over thirty find mutually compatible partners. She incorporated her social science research into the inventory, similar to the Myers-Briggs Type Indicator because, she said, "We are all interested in similar as well as complementary factors." Today this site has over seven million members.

In 2005, Pepper was recognized for her work when she received the American Sociological Award for the Public Dissemination of Information. "I was so honored because this was an award for being academically responsible. I was just so pleased to see how meaningful my work was considered."

Pepper has continued her work and contributes regularly to magazines, newspapers and journals; her work has been featured in everything from *The New York Times* to *Glamour* magazine to *Psychology Today*. She has been a regular contributor to KIRO-TV (Seattle), appears frequently on national television news, has been featured in documentaries, and recently lent her expertise to a movie.

Though Pepper Schwartz stands only four-feet, eleven inches tall, this larger-than-life woman is still, "intensely interested in sex and relationships. It's really important to take on the things that inspire you and that you find meaningful. In fact, it would kill me if I ever *un*-started."

No chance of that for this self-starter!

CHANGE YOUR THINKING; CHANGE YOUR LIFE

LOU TICE

Position: Co-Founder/Chairman, The Pacific Institute, Inc. |
Accomplishments: His message of "change your thinking" is known to millions of people around the world | **Birthplace:** WA

Lou Tice, chairman of The Pacific Institute, remains one of the world's foremost leaders in helping others reach their potential. After forty years of teaching people and traveling the globe, this sophisticated, impeccably dressed gentleman has lost none of his energy and passion.

Lou founded The Pacific Institute in Seattle, Washington in 1971 with his wife, Diane. Today, The Pacific Institute works with multinational businesses, innovative entrepreneurs, education professionals and government agencies—they all benefit from his "no limits" philosophy. Clients and the media call him everything from *guru* to *teacher extraordinaire* to *visionary* to *consummate mentor.* All designations fit.

Lou believes that "self-starters are those who are *self*-determined, not other-person-determined. If it's somebody else's goal, then you always need somebody else's energy to get you started. Self-starters are internally driven. They have their own ideas about how they want to live. They invent their own life and thus motivate themselves to achieve success." Lou has lived that motto all his adult years, but his ideas started at an early age.

"I knew intuitively when I was six that I would take care of my family. I couldn't have told you why I knew this, but I started preparing myself." When he was eight years old, he sold clusters of holly in the neighborhood during Christmastime, then moved onto paper routes at nine. By age ten, he was working on wheat and cattle ranches in Washington state. "It was on that ranch that I learned many life lessons; self-reliance being the most important one."

His persona mirrors that of a cowboy—a man who is tough, determined and self-reliant, who doesn't cry, and looks out at vast frontiers to conquer. But first, Lou had to get in the saddle. "Week Two on the ranch: I was ten and trying to saddle a horse. I could hardly reach the stirrups, but the guys in the barn just saddled up and rode off, saying, 'See ya.' It was a matter of, 'We're not gonna help you; you need to be self-reliant.' So, I had to be really creative and figure out how to throw a rope over a rafter, tie one end to the horn, lift the saddle, get the horse under, drop it down, saddle up and be off."

That self-reliance helped him after his father died and the family went on welfare. "I was twelve. I realized I could sit and whine and cry, or I could get my ass going and figure out a way to take care of all of us."

Lou's self-reliance gave him incredible maturity, even at a young age. He married his wife, Diane, when he was only eighteen. The couple raised Lou's brothers while he and Diane attended college and worked full-time. Upon graduation, Lou became a high school teacher and football coach. He continued his education, taking graduate classes on cognitive psychology at the University of Washington, where he earned his MA in mental health education. There, he learned about the power of a positive mindset.

Lou applied this theory to his athletes and football coaching style. He worked with his students to believe there were no limits to their abilities inside or outside the classroom. His players started winning games and achieving in the classroom beyond that which they had previously thought they were capable. They realized that by becoming internally motivated, they could determine the course of their lives and achieve their dreams. "When you commit to a vision, a dream, a result, the dissonance inside you motivates you to invent the way to your goals," said Lou.

Lou's philosophy, that if you change your thinking you can change your life, certainly changed his. He left teaching in 1970 and, with $1,000 in the bank and nine foster and adopted children in the house, started The Pacific Institute.

Today Lou's teachings have transformed the lives of millions of people by showing them how to reach their potential through a positive, option-seeking attitude. His prominence has taken him to some of the world's hot spots: from Northern Ireland, where he has worked with their leaders since the mid-'80s; to Guatemala, where he has worked since the signing of the Peace Accords in 1995; and to South Africa, where he started working long before the end of apartheid.

Without his positive-thinking core philosophy and belief in himself, none of his amazing feats would have been possible. "I had never stayed in a motel or flown in an airplane until I was thirty-five; I never owned a car until I was thirty-seven. I had never traveled farther than the 140 miles to the ranch." Thanks to his positive attitude and dedication to his work, Lou changed his life and the lives of those around him.

"You know how, when you're young, you make all these vows to yourself about what your life will be like when you're older? Mine was to not live like I did growing up. I wanted to live in the nicest house—not the worst—and to take care of myself.

"Interesting where your thoughts can take you, isn't it?"

KeyNotes

Self-starters possess an inner drive. As one of the self-starters in this chapter said, the world is littered with self-starters but being self-motivated is what makes the difference. No one needs to give self-starters permission to do what needs to be done; they just do it. They pull from an inner core of strength and push through, even when times are tough.

How would you answer these questions?

1. What strengths do you draw on to reach your goals?

2. What motivates you to get things done? Is it a specific project? If so, what kind of project, or what kind of opportunities does it offer?

Activities:

- Think about what would motivate you to take the next steps when an opportunity presents itself. What would those process steps be? Make them more powerful by fully identifying them.

- Write about a particular experience where you realized you were totally motivated about something and were driven to take action. What did you do? Who was involved? How did it turn out?

SIX

CREATIVITY SPARKS SOLUTIONS

Creativity: Invention; originality; ingenuity; fertile mind; prolificacy; imagination.

Creativity can be learned. It's a skill these self-starters have developed and nurtured. Some call it "thinking outside of the box"; others view it as possessing a vivid imagination; some say it's a logical process that extends past linear thinking.

OVERCOMING OBSTACLES WITH 'CREOSITY'

RON D. BARBARO

Position: Chairman/CEO, Ontario Lottery and Gaming Corporation; President, Prudential Insurance Company of America (former) |
Accomplishment: Created insurance "living needs" benefit |
Birthplace: Toronto, Canada

On a hot summer day in 1985, Ron Barbaro, then president of Prudential Insurance Company of America, walked into Casey House, a Toronto hospice for people with AIDS. He approached a young man lying in bed and said,

"Hi! I'd like to help."

"Then *help* me die with dignity!" the young man yelled.

That plea started Ron on a path that turned the traditional, highly regulated insurance industry on its head. His revolutionary idea changed how people diagnosed with a terminal disease could receive benefits and was the biggest transformation in providing insurance in 120 years. The term Ron invented, "living benefit," is now recognized throughout the industry and even defined in the dictionary. Ron's creative thinking changed the lives of very ill people by giving them the option to collect a portion of their life insurance benefits and to pay for medical bills and other personal comforts while they are still living.

He believes creativity is essential to being a self-starter. "I call it *creosity*, a term I coined. It combines the word curiosity with creativity. Curiosity leads to creativity which leads to forward action. A self-starter must have creativity to achieve anything. Creativity, combined with curiosity, will help you achieve what wasn't possible."

Ron's creosity was stimulated by his conversation with the ill man. "When that young man died, I found out he had sold everything but his shoes to pay for medicine. He had no money to even have his family come from Germany and visit him to say goodbye. He died with a $25,000 life insurance policy. That $25,000 could have paid for medication, could have eased his final days. I asked myself, 'How? How could this be?!'

"So I called a meeting of the executives: my vice presidents, medical directors, lawyers and actuaries. I asked them, 'Why couldn't these terminally ill people be given a portion of their life insurance benefits while they are still living? Why couldn't we accelerate the death benefits?'

"Everyone was stunned. They said, 'It's a hundred-year-old rule! Have you lost your mind? Why would you do something like that?! You don't have to! People die—*then* we pay!'

"It's true; there were a thousand reasons *not* to do it. One objection, for example, held that advancing a *portion* of the total death benefit should be treated as a loan, thereby not discriminating against other policyholders. The clear solution, once we thought about it, was to deduct the interest against the remaining value of the policy. It took me four days to get a consensus for a pilot program on a need-to-know basis."

After fulfilling a dozen of these claims, the chairman of the board got wind of the fact that Ron was approving claims for terminally-ill people. It was too late; the media had already jumped on the story. With appearances on ABC's *Good Morning America*, NBC's *TODAY Show*, and a televised conversation with Peter Jennings for *ABC World News Tonight*, Ron and his idea were unstoppable.

Today, worldwide, all insurance companies have a "living needs" benefit as a legitimate alternative. "I believe creativity is a renewable resource, and everyone has it. If you are curious, you can be creative," Ron said. "Creativity is sometimes a curse; I'm always thinking of other ways to do something all the time."

Another big creative coup for Ron was when he served as volunteer chairman of the Toronto Zoo and brought the first-ever Giant Panda exhibit to Canada in 1985, despite being told it was an unachievable goal. "When someone says that to me, it's like waving a red flag in front of a bull. I start thinking of all the ways I can make it happen." For Ron, his creosity creates serendipity, which creates opportunities that "you would never have thought about, and from there it creates forward movement," he enthused.

Then there was downtown Toronto's Santa Claus Parade, the world's longest-running kids' parade, and a televised event shown across North America. Eaton's, a now-defunct department store chain, had financed the parade for seventy-nine years; however, the company announced in August 1982 they would no longer be able to do so because of financial difficulties. Ron got creative and quickly worked with a friend to raise the $500,000 needed for that first post-Eaton's year. In 2010, Ron and a dedicated group of volunteers will confirm—for the twentieth-eighth time—to millions of children that Santa is recession-proof.

In 1998, after "failing retirement" three times, Ron became chairman and CEO of the Ontario Lottery and Gaming Corporation (OLGC). Under his leadership, OLGC expanded its gaming activities and profits. On the lottery side, Ron applied the insurance annuity concept and developed a lottery ticket that became the hottest scratch ticket ever, grossing hundreds of millions of dollars. The lottery and gaming revenues, when combined, generate more than $2 billion in net profits a year.

No matter what role he's in, Ron has always faced obstacles and used his creativity to overcome them. He never attended college, yet became president of the Prudential Insurance Company of America, Worldwide Operations. He received an honorary doctorate and has been inducted into both the Canadian and American Sales and Marketing Hall of Fame. Even though he grew up as a Catholic Italian-Canadian, he was recognized at Hebrew University of Jerusalem with the Ron Barbaro Chair in Veterinary Medicine for his philanthropy. In fact, Ron's list of accomplishments, achievements and accolades is pages in length. His philanthropy, business acumen and commitment to his community are legendary.

Now age 78, Ron still believes that "you'll never self-start anything if you don't have the curiosity, which naturally leads to creativity."

Breaking the Mold

Helen Chou

Position: Founder/CEO, Atomic9 Fusion Electronics |
Accomplishment: Academy Award winner; Emmy Award finalist in interactive television technology | **Birthplace:** Taiwan

GrungeBuds, RumbleBud, DJ headphones, Pico Video Projectors, Dick Tracy Bluetooth Wristband Speakerphone are all product names associated with Helen Chou's company, Atomic9 Fusion Electronics. Helen, an electrical engineer with a master's degree in image processing, is one of the coolest women in Hollywood, thanks to her exciting and unusual fashionista tech products. And that's really saying something in southern California, where some of the world's most creative minds flock to join the entertainment industry. Helen was born in Taiwan and in 1980, when she was ten, her parents sold everything they had so the family could emigrate to the U.S. They arrived with $2,000. "My dad sacrificed everything—his successful business, his homeland, his extended family—in hopes of getting a piece of the American dream; mainly, an education for us kids."

Helen vividly remembers her first day of school in America. Even though her parents had run a school teaching English in Taiwan, they had refused to teach her the language.

"My father didn't want me to have his accent," she recalled. "He was keen on making us independent, so he had taught me one sentence, 'I don't speak English.' That first day, he pulled up in front of the school, opened the car door and said, in Chinese, of course, 'Okay, God Bless, good luck and don't forget the sentence I taught you!'

"'Aren't you going to walk me to the class?' my ten-year-old self asked. He said, 'No, I want you to be independent, and figure this out for yourself,' and drove away," Helen recalled in amazement. When it came to learning the language of her new home, Helen was on her own.

She quickly discovered her teacher was willing to tutor her after school. That tutelage, along with working the flea markets with her parents, helped her quickly converse fluently in English and taught her a lot about retailing. "I've often thanked my parents for giving me such a unique opportunity," she giggled. "This goes to show that there is a silver lining to every obstacle."

"Since I was little, I've always wanted to invent things to help people—that's why I became an engineer." That's where creativity for Helen—her No. 1 attribute for any self-starter—comes into play. In Helen's opinion, "a self-starter is someone who truly believes in his or her own creative vision. Creativity is behind everything. You have to be creative to figure out how to make every aspect of your dream come true—whether it's your business, your job or just an idea that you want to grow into a full business," Helen said earnestly.

Helen put her engineering degree to work at the Jet Propulsion Labs on "rocket scientist stuff." In 1996, she was offered a doctoral fellowship at University of California, Los Angeles to continue her studies in engineering, but turned it down in order to care for her parents.

Though she was trained in the fields of engineering and technology, it was the time she worked at Warner Brothers in the late '90s that she brought together her technology expertise and her interest in the field of entertainment. "We launched DVDs worldwide." Helen's face lit up as she described the new outlet for her creativity. "In the wake of the new digital media paradigm, I got to work on all the exciting projects, such as video-on-demand, interactive television and digital Internet television."

In addition to working with Warner Brothers, Helen launched many other companies. "I created several startups within the motion picture industry, working with studios—always focused on introducing new technologies." Helen loved her work, but the crazy pace finally took its toll. "I was in Europe working twenty hours a day [she was running a company that had won an Academy Award in 2007 as co-producer of *The Last King of Scotland* and was an Emmy finalist before that] and I said to myself, 'I'm not happy. I'm lonely. This isn't fun. I'm not following my dream. I want to do my own thing.'" Helen came home to Los Angeles to start her childhood dream.

After two years of brainstorming, strategic planning, research and development, Helen was ready with the vision—she launched Atomic9 Fusion Electronics, where she combines her engineering background with her creative sensibilities. "I love the inspiration that comes out of mixing different ideas. I'm a combination of different things. I'm Asian, a woman and an engineer, and I was an Asian running an American company in Europe."

She used that same philosophy to develop her company's award-winning products, including her consumer electronics. "Why not combine fashion with technology?" she thought. "There's synergy around putting together opposites, like fashion and technology. Technology does not need to be boring, serious or male-centric."

Her premise was "to break the mold and create something new and exciting. People often are intimidated by technology. A phone, for example, is typically seen as a piece of technology that brings people together. So essentially it's a socially enabling technology—so why not make it less intimidating, more personal, more of a reflection of your style and habits? So why not make it into a bracelet? a necklace? Then it becomes truly a part of our modern lifestyle to be fully immersed and enjoyed."

"It's like a fruit salad—I take opposite elements and put all the pieces together to create cool stuff. You can make a pretty good fruit salad that way!"

Her advice to readers: "Always follow your dreams, but don't forget the detailed planning—It's like making sure you have your parachute when you take off with your new ideas."

New Models to Fix Old Problems

Lori Pappas

Position: Founder/Chairman, Global Team for Local Initiatives |
Accomplishment: Established an organization to work with the last
indigenous tribe in Ethiopia to regain its self-reliance and ability to
survive | **Birthplace:** MN

For much of the year, Lori Pappas lives in a tent in the arid lowlands
of Ethiopia. Why? In order to help the Hamar, an ancient tribe that
has virtually no contact with the modern world.

Lori first met the Hamar in 2007 while doing volunteer work in
the area and was disturbed by the group's fragility. Facing devastating drought and disease, they desperately needed outside help—from
creative thinkers—to survive, but no one was offering the sustainable
assistance they needed. So Lori decided she would.

She'd already founded, grown and sold a highly successful software
company, JobBOSS Software; now she wanted to apply her entrepreneurial mindset, business skills and outside-the-box thinking to the
intractable challenges of international development. Her goal was not to

deliver aid to the tribe, but to help them develop the skills they needed to become self-reliant.

The only problem was how to do that? The models of development Lori had seen struck her as unsustainable. "Handing out vitamins and de-worming pills does nothing long-term," she said. "That only makes people dependent. And putting in wells only supplies water until the well breaks."

For the Hamar to become self-reliant, they would need to *own* their solutions. Western solutions, imposed from outside, would never work. Whatever the solution would be, it was clear that a creative, unorthodox process was needed to save the tribe.

"I knew I couldn't come in with a prescribed answer," she said. "I had to start with questions. And the biggest question was, 'What is the ultimate result I'm looking for?' The answer was to help these people lead a healthy life, which is incredibly complex. So I knew I had to be willing to answer it by thinking way outside the box." So Lori began the process of getting to know the tribe—forming relationships, building trust, asking questions—and mostly listening to the answers.

Others recognized Lori's ability to think outside the box early in her life. Hired right out of high school to organize a file room, she was promoted within three days to bookkeeping, where she computerized the company's systems. In every subsequent job, she systemized processes and solved productivity issues.

When Olivetti Corporation hired her in the late 1970s, she promptly became one of their top salespeople in the country. "By then, I had a clear understanding of the user experience, so I could help customers with their issues," she said. That experience gave her the wherewithal to start her own software company in 1984. "I was lucky. I was a single mom with two little girls. My father had given them $3,000 each, but he made the mistake of making me the trustee. I took the money and started the business!"

That gamble paid off. Over the next twenty years, JobBOSS Software became one of *Inc.* magazine's "Best Small Companies to Work For," and Lori was named Entrepreneur of the Year by the Minnesota High

Tech Association in recognition of her personal philosophy and her ability to challenge paradigms.

In 1999, she sold the company and retired. That didn't last long.

"I failed retirement," she laughed. Lori was more drawn to the heartbreaking problems she'd seen on numerous trips to Africa than to a lifestyle of golf and leisure. And she was convinced her creativity and systems skills would serve well in tackling the continent's challenges. So she started another company: the Global Team for Local Initiatives.

"I put my energy into figuring out what I could do to make a difference. But the traditional ways of solving problems don't work here because the problems are so complex. We're working with cultural barriers, socioeconomic barriers; plus malnutrition and dehydration, shrinking grazing grounds, no knowledge of the national language, no writing system, no system of counting above ten, no accurate sense of time, no transportation other than by foot, no electricity," she explained.

The only way to solve the problems would be to do exactly what Lori did in software: understand the "user's experience" thoroughly and then engage them in developing the solutions.

Hence the years of living in the tent, questioning, observing and talking endlessly with elders about why the traditional ways of Hamar life no longer keep the tribe alive. Gradually, as trust grew, Lori and the elders agreed on programs that GTLI and the tribe could work on together to improve the community's health.

First was creating a line of Hamar products based on the beaded jewelry they wear; GTLI could sell the products in the West to create an income stream that would enable the tribe to purchase food. Second—and far more challenging—was replacing the longstanding behaviors of open-field defecation and a general lack of hygiene with the use of pit latrines and hand washing. Changing behaviors would be dauntingly difficult but essential if the tribe was to become healthy. The elders agreed to support and model the new behaviors.

Today, Lori splits her time between the Ethiopian capital, Addis Ababa, and her tent in Hamar woreda. Hamar "community facilitators" have been trained to lead small group discussions in which members identify problems and determine appropriate solutions. This tact is working. Tribe members are coming to understand that organisms they cannot see are making them sick. Eventually, these small discussion groups will use peer pressure to elicit behavior changes among their members. Meanwhile, trial sales of Hamar belts and bracelets in the West suggest that, after a little refinement, a viable line of Hamar accessories may be possible.

Progress will come slowly, Lori knows. "In addition to creativity, you need incredible patience, and that's not easy for a former Type-A personality like me! But for the first time in my life, I'm learning not just to do, but to *be*. And that is really a gift."

MEDICAL BOOKS AND MARITAL AFFAIRS

LANA STAHELI

Position: Psychotherapist; Co-Founder of Global HELP; Founder/President, The Rainier Foundation | **Accomplishment:** Author; Founder, Bounce Be Transformed; recipient of Community Stars and Heroes Award from Children's Hospital, Seattle | **Birthplace:** MI

When people say to Dr. Lana Staheli, "Wow, you're such an out-of-the-box thinker," she responds, "I didn't even know there was a box." Lana's life has always been and remains one of transformation and re-creation—not just for her, but for the thousands of lives she has touched.

This medical secretary-turned-counselor-turned-life-coach-turned-author-turned-philanthropist has reinvented herself several times. She attributes her amazing success with life's twists and turns to her unconventional thinking. "Self-starters transcend. They think in new ways. The very act of creativity breathes new life into your world and takes you beyond where you presently reside," she said.

Guiding people to imagine their lives differently has been her life path, despite her own difficulties.

Lana was born with a birth defect that's typically fatal. "I was one of the first babies to ever survive the birth defect known as TE Fistula: my esophagus went into my lungs instead of my stomach at birth. Today, I have limited lung capacity and a little heart defect and I have no peristalisis. I rely completely on gravity to swallow everything." Despite the severity of her condition, Lana refused to be victimized. "Life is difficult sometimes. So what? Get over it and move on—that's what I tell myself."

When Lana was in elementary school, her teacher told her that she was *not college material but would be a lovely homemaker.* "Granted, I wasn't a straight-A student. I had five surgeries as an infant, and in those days they used ether as anesthesia and there had been concern that my brain might have been damaged from all the procedures. After some psychological testing, I decided I probably wasn't *that smart* but I wasn't retarded either. My only A in high school was in home economics, thus the 'lovely homemaker' comment. And, incidentally, I think it's really funny I was given that label because I don't do any of those home economics things like cooking, housecleaning or sewing," she smiled.

She didn't even consider college when she graduated high school. Instead, she went to school to be a medical secretary. Seven years and two marriages later, Lana found her calling. "I wanted to be a psychotherapist counselor. I got a PhD in psychology, started my practice and began raising three stepchildren." Lana was only twenty-five when she started her practice and twenty-nine years old when she inherited three stepchildren.

In 1970, she began her private therapy practice in Seattle, working with clients who were highly successful. Some of her clients were dealing with adulterous partners, and she knew couples would either choose to reinvent themselves and their marriages in an attempt to stay together—or some would not. To help her clients, she wrote a booklet, *Triangles, Facts on Affairs,* which led to a media interview, then to a syndicated article and books, and eventually to radio and television talk shows. She became known as the "Queen of Infidelity." Though her therapy practice focuses on more than helping people get through emotional turmoil, Lana wanted people to see personal growth as a lifelong learning process, to find joy in becoming their personal best and to exercise their creativity. In 1983, she started The Rainier Foundation with a group of eight other young professionals. This non-profit echoed Lana's philosophy of supporting people who think outside of the box and make a difference in their communities.

Lana also applies her belief of going beyond conventional thinking to effectively tackle global issues. In 2002, she and her husband co-founded the groundbreaking Global HELP, a non-profit organization to produce and distribute free or low-cost textbooks congruent with the native language, equipment, medical practices and cultural mores of each of the third-world countries they help. "This had never been done before. We were breaking new ground and creatively problem-solving how to produce publications sensitive to each country's culture," she says proudly.

Today, countries around the world receive accurate, professional and affordable textbooks, thanks to Lana's abilities to creatively problem solve. Global HELP has provided 60 free publications, some of which were translated into 15 or more languages, with new publications added all the time. Over 250,000 pdf publications have been downloaded from the non-profit's website to individuals in over 150 countries. In addition, more than 60 countries have received 20,000 printed publications.

In 2007, Lana started an endowment at Seattle Children's Hospital to give back to the health workers who had been so instrumental in saving her life as an infant and child. Her endowment funds programs on personal growth and supports inspirational lectures. "I want the money to be used to help medical staff focus on life outside of medicine," she says, "because when time and opportunity open up, creativity rushes in."

Lana has always faced her obstacles with levity. "Self-starters run into hard things along the way, but they bounce like a ball and re-create themselves. They find solutions, they become better . . . they bounce!"

Lana used this philosophy as the basis for her newest creation and 2008 book, *Bounce Be Transformed*, now in its third printing. She explained, "When a ball is fully inflated, it is well-rounded and it bounces. It has energy. It may be a bit unpredictable, but it is lively and fun. When life is well-rounded, our needs are met, friends like to be around us and we have fun. Joy and purpose are part of everyday life, and we have Bounce!"

Based on her book, Lana created Bounce groups for women over forty; the groups abound all over the Puget Sound. Lana's message to women is one of hope. "You can Bounce and reinvent yourself. You can go beyond where you're been before. You must have a willingness to change, to embrace your creativity. Or you can choose to sit in your garden with your dog and wait to die.

"For me, I am willing to leave the groove. I find joy and growth in seeking new experience and new adventures," she said with a satisfied smile.

Pulling Rabbits Out of Hats Takes Discipline

Jonathan Todd

Position: Owner, Jonathan Todd Productions | **Accomplishment:** Branded, marketed and sold Mick Fleetwood Private Cellar wine to Costco and achieved that company's highest gross sales for any celebrity product; credited for creating the new rules of "star marketing and branding" by branching celebrities out of their conventional roles | **Birthplace:** CA

A fencer, a general, a magician—Jonathan Todd encompasses all three personas. His marketing genius allows him to parry and thrust when necessary, to take command and run marketing campaigns, and to pull a rabbit out of a hat when required. Discipline is the fuel for his creative energy.

Jonathan's unusual background honed his unique skill sets. In 1975, as a fifteen-year-old, he was invited to join The Magic Castle, the world's most famous club for magicians. As a junior magician, he beat out hundreds of applicants for twenty-three slots held out to the most accomplished youngsters. That entré connected Jonathan with a group founded by brilliant science fiction and futuristic writers Isaac Asimov and Aldous Huxley, as well as astronomer and astrophysicist

Carl Sagan. This group, called the Committee for Scientific Investigation into the Claims of the Paranormal (CSICOP), sent Jonathan and others out to look at "paranormal incidences—to debunk or, in some cases, to reach no conclusion. It was an interesting group of very intellectual people to be hanging out with at my age. We would get an assignment from the Air Force, for example, to look into something that had no explanation, or someone else would have us check out ghost stories or paranormal stuff—all kinds of unusual scenarios."

"These experiences were the beginning roots of what made me sort of different as an adult," Jonathan admitted, grinning.

His college education ended abruptly his senior year when his business professor screamed at his students that if they didn't become better communicators they wouldn't even make $30,000 a year.

Jonathan asked himself that day, "Hmm. I'm making triple that doing magic shows at conventions, so . . . why do I want my degree?" Retelling the story, he chuckled as he continued, "The decision to leave school was easy; my only worry was if I had any library books that were due."

With hubris and naiveté, Jonathan decided his best career move would be to join the Air Force as a captain. "I offered them my expertise and suggested I just bypass basic training and start as an officer. Their response was 'No, thank you!' I found this very hard to believe," he smiled.

Undiscouraged, he approached a cruise line. "Again, when I suggested they hire me to run their marketing and sales department, they also said no. This really upset me!"

Jonathan was not to be deterred. He had had his eye on a national cruise director position. He talked his way on board a ship where the cruise line president was staying. Using his creativity and magician chops, he rigged the vessel with magic gear and "entertained my way into their hearts." He landed the job.

With several marketing jobs under his belt, Jonathan's remarkable ingenuity came into play when he was assigned to create and sell the vision of a cruise ship that had not yet been built. "I had to leave a stirring impression of reality and build a confidence level high enough to book clients. We did not disappoint—except that, on the maiden voyage, the boat sank!" With clever thinking, Jonathan turned the disaster into something positive and had people signing up for the next cruise. "I called the media and gave access to the sinking ship. It made global news and in days people were at travel agencies and picking up a brochure. About 10 percent said, "Isn't that the boat company that just sank one?" while the other 90 percent were saying, "Hmm . . . I've heard of them before, let's go!"

Jonathan's early forays into the corporate world clearly demonstrate his definition: "Creativity is what self-starters thrive on. Self-starters create their own scenarios in which they can live and work in ways that best meet their needs and foster creative thought," explained Jonathan. "But," he cautioned, "without the discipline to carry out those creative ideas, all is lost. I call it the necessary combination of the "fencer" (employing the mental and physical aspects of chess), the "general" (understanding the past and thinking futuristically), and the "magician" (putting a new twist on an idea)."

Jonathan's creativity—mated with a disciplined approach—contributed to the systematizing of his unique sales process and the creation of a business that produced and sold what he has coined sales "Semestinars" (half a seminar, half a semester in length) nationally and internationally. "We grew so fast, I was killing myself and couldn't manage the growth. On top of that, we did not get paid for a large international contract—so, ultimately, I went bankrupt. I was still in my twenties and went from living the high life to going as low as you can go."

The best was yet to come. Jonathan became involved with promoting talented artists and started another business, Sabre Entertainment. He began managing the marketing, licensing and branding for Mick Fleetwood of the musical group Fleetwood Mac, and co-managed his Island Rumours Band and The Mick Fleetwood Blues Band. Under Todd's guidance, the blues band went on to receive a Grammy Nomination in 2010, the first Mick has received for any project other than Fleetwood Mac.

Later, Jonathan called on all three of his personas—the fencer, the general and the magician—for his "Costco coup," as he calls it. The story goes like this: Mick Fleetwood liked good wines and wanted to be able to order the wine he liked from anywhere in the world and be assured it would have the same consistency and taste. Jonathan decided to honor his client's request. But rather than investing in a vineyard, Jonathan convinced Mick he'd have more freedom and control by blending *what* he wanted with *who* he wanted to work with. Again, with more outside-the-box ingenuity, this became the first "vineyard-independent" celebrity wine.

"That concept riled up the wine industry—comments like 'Impossible!' and 'It can't be done!' and 'People want *terroir*,' and 'Who's Mick Fleetwood, some grand vintner!?' were commonplace. Yet, ten years later, we were the success story of the decade for this concept, with featured stories in *Wine Enthusiast* and *Wine Connoisseur*," Jonathan smiled wryly.

Starting small and building the brand, they first approached local, high-end southern California markets. "It was a huge success," he says matter-of-factly. "We had 2,000 people lined up to get the wine and Mick's autograph! They had to call in security and there were news helicopters flying overhead."

With that victory, Costco was the next stop and Jonathan repeated the process. "We started with product in four stores, put our muscle into it and got thousands of people coming into the stores to buy the wine. The trick was in the public relations and communications, which I did through my own company rather than farming it out. We controlled every PR move, including the Internet social media and the Costco presentation, in great detail," said Todd. "We moved millions and millions of dollars of wine through Costco." The end result: "We outsold Oprah on her book signings, we outsold Colin Powell and we outsold the Clintons. We still have the record for the highest gross sales for any celebrity product," he says with pride, and rightfully so.

Creativity is the well-known hallmark of his success, but Jonathan also recognizes—and nurtures—the discipline behind his creative juice.

KeyNotes

Self-starters think outside the box. Though they may not necessarily be creative in the arts, they use ideas to creatively problem-solve or make decisions or create a new product or service or even, these days, a killer app.

Write answers to these questions:

1. Where are you stuck and stale in your life? Is your "box" too full of clutter?

2. What aspect or thing in your life needs more creativity?

3. How do you "spark" ideas and get your creativity going?

4. What would more creativity mean for your life, and for your work?

Activities:

- Look at the ordinary, everyday things in a new way. Drive home a different way to stimulate your brain. Move furniture or art around in your office to get a new perspective.

- Take a vacation or staycation; rest and renew. Go for a walk. Do something physical to clear your mind.

- Create folders about various ideas you have. Every time something comes to mind, capture it and put it in the folder. Go online to find articles which might stimulate additional ideas around an aspect of your life you know lacks creativity.

Seven

Risk-Taking Reaps Rewards

Risk-taking: Adventuresome; daring; audacious; enterprising; intrepid; bold; brave.

Risk-takers are often described as those who jump off cliffs and grow wings as they fall. Though there may be some truth to this adage, these risk-takers view risk as part of the price of living, of working, of creating. Staying safe all the time will not produce the results you desire; deliberate risk may just get you there.

RISK TAKING IS ACTUALLY MORE LIKE . . . READY, FIRE, AIM!

PHYLLIS CAMPBELL

Position: Chairman, Pacific Northwest Region, JPMorgan Chase |
Accomplishment: President (former) of U.S. Bank; doubled the
assets in six years as CEO of her state's largest non-profit, The Seattle
Foundation | **Birthplace:** Spokane, WA

Phyllis Campbell is a study in contrasts. Though tiny in stature, she's
played football with the guys; despite being tapped as a chairman of
a bank that employs 200,000 people, she still cleans up after staff meetings. Though she's self-assured, she is also humble enough to turn to
others for guidance. She uses her head to run the bank, yet leads with
her heart in her community-outreach activities.

Being a self-starter is all about contrasts, Phyllis said, and she
thrives on them.

Phyllis was born in Spokane, Washington, where her family lived
since her Japanese grandparents' release from internment after World
War II. "We just didn't discuss much about that discrimination. It was
hard for my grandparents to even talk about the fact that their family

was forcibly taken to these camps," she said softly. The message, passed down from grandparent to parent to Phyllis, was to achieve, to be educated, to be a good American, to be a good citizen. "They taught me how to turn a negative experience into an opportunity in order to become exemplary."

That message went along with her grandfather's wise words, "Life is not about you. It's about being an instrument for greater things." That sentiment remains the primary theme in her life.

Phyllis is a risk-taker; a measured one, but a risk-taker all the same. "That's the scary thing about being a self-starter," she said. "Risk requires you to be uncomfortable. It requires you to move ahead anyway. If you aren't a little bit scared, a little bit nervous, a little bit uncertain about the outcome, then you're probably not going to experience the stretch, the growth. But you just gotta do it."

In her career, taking risks became a way of life for Phyllis. After finishing college in the early 1970s, she applied to work at banks. Back then, very few young Asian women even tried to enter any sort of manager trainee program in the field of banking. "I was turned down. They would say, 'Gee, we don't hire women into our training programs. We hired one woman and she quit because she was pregnant. It was a bad investment.' It made me mad. I told them I'm just going to persist. So I just became a pest. I called every single day to ask, 'Are you gonna hire me or not?'"

She eventually landed that bank job and rose quickly through the ranks, from branch manager to regional manager and on to her first risky opportunity. "My boss's boss came to me and said, 'I am firing your boss in the morning and I need you to move to Seattle.' 'Whoa,' I thought to myself, 'I have a responsible job, I've settled nicely into my life, I live in such a comfortable box, why would I do that?!'

"I asked him, 'How much time do I have to decide?' He looked at his watch. 'About two hours.'"

Phyllis took the plunge, and it was onward and upward from there. Two years later, she became president of U.S. Bank of Washington. She stayed in that position for eight years, until 2001.

By then, she was ready to spend more time focusing on her grandfather's words about being an instrument for greater things. She accepted a position in the non-profit world as the CEO of The Seattle Foundation, the largest non-profit foundation in the state and among the top twenty in the country.

"I really took a risk because this job was totally out of the box for me. Something outside the scope of my vision. This was a real self-starter opportunity. I could become a self-starter in a whole new field. The risk was that I didn't know if I would be successful. I had to stretch, learn and be a leader in a very different world."

Phyllis knew she could now start to pay it forward and take philanthropy to a new level. In her six years at the foundation, charitable assets doubled to $676 million a year.

But fate came knocking on her door seven years later when, once again, she had the opportunity to take a risk. She was asked to help reverse the damage Washington Mutual Bank's demise had done to the region.

In 2009 she accepted the position as the Pacific Northwest chairman for JPMorgan Chase, the bank that bought Washington Mutual's assets in 2008.

"It's the biggest job and the biggest risk yet—to turn around a community's fury so people embrace the new kid in town. I don't take irresponsible risks, but I realized that whenever I've stretched, it's always been the right thing to do. In the end, you have to pull the trigger. That's the hard part, but sometimes the risk outweighs the reward. It's the self-starter within you that makes you do this, even when it feels a lot like 'ready . . . fire . . . aim!'"

NOT RELYING ON HIS ALARM CLOCK

TOM DOUGLAS

Position: Owner/Founder of four restaurants; creator of food products; cookbook author | **Accomplishment:** Numerous "Best" awards from James Beard and *Bon Appetit* magazine; put Seattle on the map with his Pacific Northwest Cuisine in the late '80s | **Birthplace:** DE

With thirty-plus years in the food business you'd think Tom Douglas would rest on his laurels, but this food phenom is just getting started. "I'm getting ready to risk everything we have again," he explained, so excited he couldn't sit still. "We're planning to open a group of five new restaurants. So, it's like, if you're not willing to bet the farm at some point, you must be dead."

Tom's work history in the early years reads like that of most young people, but with a few extra twists. "I did all the typical jobs as a kid. You know, a newspaper route, caddying at a golf course. But I also worked in a liquor store during high school and then on the back of a garbage truck, and finally at a railroad car repair yard," Tom said. His first restaurant job opportunity came as a cook's helper at Hotel du Pont in Delaware in 1964. "It was a great experience in a high-end place because I was exposed to all different levels of cooking."

Tom eventually got restless with his job and so, in 1978, he left Delaware in an old 1967 Chevy station wagon and headed west. "I knew I didn't want to go to college, so I drove around the country, cooking in different restaurants, and finally landed in Seattle at thirty-two years old."

He paid his dues by cooking in various restaurants, sold wine wholesale, met his future wife and business partner, Jackie, and then opened his first restaurant, Dahlia Lounge, in 1989. "We didn't have a dime; we borrowed it all. But within five years, we returned the original loan to Jackie's uncle, giving him a six-figure return on his investment," he smiled.

"You know, I'm the kind of person who just gets things done. That's how self-starters rise to the top of an organization—they just do it. And when the time was right, I went for it with our first restaurant," Tom said.

Tom's belief—if you are not risking, you are not living—has played out for him in exciting ways. He opened his second restaurant, Etta's Seafood in 1995. "We had to sign our life away again to get that place opened," said Tom, "but without pain, no gain."

The next year, Palace Kitchen opened, earning him a James Beard Foundation Award nomination (dubbed the Oscars of the food world by *Time* magazine) for Best New Restaurant. Not surprisingly, *The New York Times*, the *Los Angeles Times* and *Gourmet* magazine have all recognized his talent.

"The question I get asked most often when I say I am going to risk once again and open another restaurant is 'How many is enough for you?'" explained Tom. "I think that a sense of curiosity goes along with the risk-taking. There is a curiosity about always doing something novel. Part of risking is innovating, stepping out on a limb to try something new."

Thus he became a pioneer in using local ingredients in combination with Washington wines. "It had not really been tried before!" he said, still excited. He also discovered that no one was doing much with crab. "Here, where Dungeness crab was king, the restaurants were doing little with it!"

That didn't sit well with Tom so he experimented with different recipes and concoctions—and still does today. In return, his crab cakes remain one of the top-selling dishes in his restaurants.

Besides his restaurants, he's written several cookbooks, started a catering company, opened a bakery, created sauces and spice rubs, does a talk-radio show and even appeared on and won an episode of the *Iron Chef America* reality television show in 2005.

"I think the biggest thing I've learned from my past—and I've matured enough to recognize it—is that many people want to be managed rather than be the manager of their own lives." Wise words, and certainly an attitude that separates self-starters from others.

To Tom, a self-starter is "someone who knows how to use an alarm clock. You'd be surprised how many people tell you the alarm didn't go off and that's why they are late for work. Self-starters get out of bed and get started," he said forcefully. Tom is still leaping out of bed—with or without an alarm. In 2009, he partnered with Amazon.com to create an exclusive line of cooking and dining products. But he didn't stop there, as he is keenly aware and committed to giving back to the community; local senior centers, park departments and food banks benefit from Tom's generosity and joie de vivre. He even won an award for Outstanding Philanthropic Small Business. "I believe that I've always wanted to raise the tide for all within the community."

Though Tom may thrive on risk-taking and curiosity, don't be misled into thinking he doesn't understand the restaurant and food business—on the contrary, he is keenly aware. "I like the business of business as much as the business of food. If you're losing money every month, what's the point? At the end of the day, you have to answer the question: Did I or did I not make a living?"

From Public Assistance to Public Service

Joni Earl

Position: CEO, Sound Transit | **Accomplishment:** Turned a troubled transportation agency with a $1 billion overrun on a key project into a growing organization with a healthy balanced budget and 18.8 million riders per year | **Birthplace:** WA

Her senior year at Washington State University loomed near, and Joni Earl was flat broke. She'd worked one or two jobs for years to pay all her own college costs and looked forward to being the first one in her family to earn a degree. But carrying twenty-one credits made it nigh on impossible to hold a job that paid much.

She finally resorted to public assistance, although the humiliation weighed heavily on Joni. "My family had never been on welfare. We were always tight for money but not like this!" she said, rolling her eyes. She badly wanted that degree, however, and was willing to risk her pride.

Joni's defining moment came at 5:30 a.m. on a February day in 1975 in Pullman, Washington, where the temperature hovered at eight degrees. Embarrassed, and standing in line on cold pavement trying to get food stamps one more time, she said to herself, "I will never in my life *ever* be reliant on other people for my income. I will always support myself!"

Meanwhile, there was a family meeting in Bremerton. Her grandparents took out a small home-mortgage loan to give her $750. "That gave me enough to get by; no more food stamps. Thanks to that money, plus a little from my parents, I graduated that summer," Joni said. She immediately went to work paying her family back for the loans.

Then providence stepped in. To celebrate graduation, several girlfriends convinced Joni to take a short vacation with them to Reno, Nevada; her family urged her to go too. "I had budgeted exactly $20 a day for everything, because we were staying at a friend's house," she explained, still proud of the strict budget she'd set and stuck to. On her last night, Joni played keno cards. "I always just played the same numbers." With three dollars left and no wins, her friends called to her impatiently, "Let's go!" Just then, Joni won the jackpot—$750—which was the exact amount she owed her grandparents. In a city that thrives on risk, Joni carefully weighed the risks, gambled and won. The risks paid off—literally.

"I have been blessed with little guardian angels that appear just about the time I need them," she smiled. She's needed those guardian angels a lot in her life.

Joni has spent her twenty-five-year career in government, where she finds joy and passion in serving the public. Though we don't often think of bureaucrats as risk-takers, that's been Joni's *modus operandi* from day one. At the start of new jobs, she jumps in and undergoes trial by fire. "I call them 'stretch jobs'—they were always more than I expected or understood, but I just took a risk."

One of her first jobs, in the treasurer's office of the City of Bremerton, Washington, exemplifies her definition of risk-taking. About a year into it, the position of city treasurer opened. Those interested were required to take the civil service test. "Three of us took the test, and I ranked a high second," she said. "I felt pretty good about that, since I was competing against much older people with a lot more experience.

However, when I reviewed my scores, I found they had made an error; my cumulative score should have been higher.

"I took a risk and challenged it," she said. "They corrected the score, and I placed first—and got the new job. I then had seventeen people working for me, and I was only twenty-two years old! Trust me, people weren't interested in having someone my age run the office," she smiled. Joni looked at it as a great training ground—on how to work with people when you are young and inexperienced and also how to handle a crisis. "The city installed a new computer system. That was a disaster; we couldn't even get out the water bills!" she said.

That successful risk started Joni on an unplanned management track. Every job since has been a leadership position. "Even with my background in accounting, I knew what I really loved was the people side of things. I knew I couldn't just spend all my time with my head down in a spreadsheet."

In 1986, her accumulated skills were put to the test when she took over as city manager for a newly incorporated city. With four managers in four years, "they'd had a bit of a tumultuous time. I learned later that the city council debated behind the scenes about hiring me, because they thought I was too young, at thirty-two. But they ended up voting for me anyway. When I arrived, they hadn't learned yet how to make Mill Creek a city. My four and a half years there were a stabilizing time, and I really helped establish the foundation of the city," she said proudly. Another risk taken; another triumph.

Joni took several stretch jobs before she jumped into "the biggest, hottest frying pan she could find," when she accepted the job to be Sound Transit's first chief operating officer in 2000. Sound Transit's charge was to build a mass transit system in the Puget Sound consisting of express buses, new commuter rail and new light rail.

Immediately, the executive director asked Joni to review one of Sound Transit's most critical projects: to build a twenty-one-mile stretch of new light rail along Puget Sound's I-5 corridor. She discovered the project was $1 billion over budget and three years behind schedule. Sound Transit was quickly becoming known as a "train wreck."

"Everyone's career and reputation were on the line, from the mayor to three county executives to the Sound Transit board. The U.S. Department of Transportation was really angry and our U.S. Senator Patty Murray wasn't very pleased, especially since she had helped us get the necessary federal funding. Needless to say, morale was very bad," she sighed.

But Joni dug in and for five months worked seven days a week, eighteen hours a day. She even had some twenty-four-hour days, when her husband brought her a change of clothes. Under Joni's leadership, the Sound Transit board reexamined the project and her team revamped the cost system and decision processes. "Sometimes during the wee, dark hours of the night, and with other people on the staff working alongside me, I asked myself, 'What am I doing?' I had never been tested like this before. I didn't know if I had the capacity or capability to do this." This was her biggest risk to date.

It took a while, but she and her hard-working team persevered and triumphed. In July 2009, Sound Transit opened its first fourteen miles of light rail service. By December 2009, the line was extended another 1.9 miles to the Seattle-Tacoma Airport. Under Joni's continued leadership, Sound Transit now serves over eighteen million riders annually with buses, commuter trains and light rail. And, most notably, the voters regained their trust in Sound Transit's ability to deliver; they voted in 2008 to raise their taxes to help pay for a 36-mile light rail expansion and additional transit projects.

Some people would say that this might be a good time to leave. "I'm not ready yet," Joni said with satisfaction. She knows more risks lie ahead and she's there to greet them.

Taking Risks and Enjoying the Consequences

Jeff Smulyan

Position: Founder/CEO, Emmis Communications | **Accomplishment:** Named one of 10 most influential radio executives in previous two decades by *Radio Ink* magazine; negotiated a landmark telecommunications agreement between Israel and the PLO | **Birthplace:** IN

Career aspirations as a young person often lead to interesting outcomes. Jeff Smulyan, media mogul, smiles as he ticks off the list of things he thought he was destined to do.

"I thought I was going to play center field for the San Francisco Giants but it was rather apparent early on that I wasn't talented enough." Yet Jeff owned a major league baseball team for several years.

He thought he was going to be a lawyer . . . and when that didn't turn out to be his career path, he still earned his law degree and has since used his legal knowledge to start, buy, sell and operate many businesses, including twenty-five radio stations.

He was certain that once he left his home state, he would never return. Yet he is consistently recognized for his humanitarian efforts and business acumen in Indiana, an unlikely headquarters for a media empire.

Jeff Smulyan, a man who took risks each time he's reinvented himself—and soared higher because of it—has a lot to say about self-starters.

"Whenever I speak to college graduates, I always say, 'Look, go out there and be prepared to fail—because life involves risk-taking.' They always laugh, and I retort, 'I'm serious. How you deal with risk and adversity, how persistent and resilient you are, will be the measure of your success—absolutely, positively.' I've never met a successful person who did not fail."

Jeff would tell you risk-taking is a key ingredient for a self-starter. His recipe is complex. "To risk your reputation, time, resources and your future, you have to believe in something, be passionate about something, to have success. It's multi-layered. You have to be passionate to get up every day and go for it. Without persistence you can't make it over the hurdles. Without resilience you can't bounce back from the curve balls—excuse the baseball reference—you're thrown. The ability to persevere and to do so passionately is essential. That's how you can take a risk and get results."

Jeff became enamored with radio while listening to baseball games and rock 'n roll as a youth. "When my baseball career didn't pan out, I realized it was radio—originally just a hobby—that I really wanted to do!" he said. So he majored in telecommunications at the University of Southern California and worked summers for ABC Radio in Los Angeles and as a sports writer for an Indianapolis newspaper.

After graduation in 1973, Jeff acted on a promise to himself—to own a radio station—but, initially, he met with little success. An opportunity presented itself back in his hometown and he returned to run a small station in which his father had invested. "Finally, I was on the road to my dream. This stop was fun. I learned a lot, gained an enormous amount of experience, met interesting people, and in fact, my first midday guy was David Letterman," he grinned.

Jeff had ideas—unconventional ideas—about what would work in radio. He knew preternaturally that AM stations were going to be the province of talk radio, not music. He took the risk and started his own radio station in the late 1970s with that in mind.

He still faced tremendous challenges to realize his dream: a two-year battle to get his radio tower built, regulatory hurdles, conflicts with the FAA (which was in conflict with a state agency—"It was a nightmare!" said Jeff), zoning problems, and friends and family saying, "Why don't you give this up?!"

Jeff said to them, "This is my dream. Sure, it's a big risk, but I will never quit."

Risky business, to build a radio station from scratch and against this much opposition, but Jeff knew the results would be worth it—he would accomplish his goal.

Once he was up and running, the next obstacle loomed, which was to sell his creation, the first-ever all-talk radio sports station, to listeners. "People said, 'What are you doing?' But the response was amazing; it became a powerhouse," he said proudly. After that success, he tried an all hip-hop station, the first one ever. "Once again, people said we were completely crazy. But the format really took off." And, once again, his risks paid off. "You can't always follow conventional wisdom. You have to challenge it, risk it, to succeed," he said emphatically.

And succeed he did. His current stable of media, besides radio stations, includes magazine publishing with operations in ten U.S. markets, as well as in Bulgaria and Slovakia.

His business, Emmis Communications, has had "lots of ups and lots of downs," but Jeff has faced them with an optimism that defied the reality staring him in the face. The 1980s recession, the ill-fated 1989 purchase of the Seattle Mariners (which he sold three years later), the economic downturn of 2009—through it all, Jeff just kept moving forward . . . risks and all. "You can't achieve anything unless you take a risk. Sometimes you may be wrong, but the idea is to be right more often than wrong!" he concluded.

"Besides, anyone who has played golf with me knows *that's* not a career alternative," he joked.

IGNORING THE NAYSAYERS; TAKING THE RISK

KENT STOWELL AND FRANCIA RUSSELL

Position: Artistic Directors, Pacific Northwest Ballet | **Accomplishment:** Revitalized the dance company and school; produced groundbreaking *Nutcracker* with author/artist Maurice Sendak; received honorary doctorates, University of Washington, 2010 | **Birthplace:** ID/CA

"If we'd wavered, it would have all fallen apart," said Francia Russell, as she and husband—and fellow artistic director of the Pacific Northwest Ballet—Kent Stowell described the series of risks they took that put them where they are today: twenty-eight-year veteran directors of what was a small, struggling organization when they agreed to run it. "It was in its infancy in 1977; there were no dancers and the small school was a free-for-all," Francia elaborated.

Today, it is internationally recognized as a top ballet company and school and boasts the highest per-capita attendance in the United States. The more than 200 ballets, re-stagings and new productions the couple has produced gave Pacific Northwest Ballet a new lease on life and skyrocketed it to national fame and attention.

But had this couple of nearly fifty years shied away when they faced risks throughout their lives, their success would never have happened.

"We somehow believed that we could do this . . . it was nothing about self-confidence or ego. It was just that we had set ourselves this task and the two of us—when no one else was with us—had blinders on and just naively believed we could do it," said Francia.

Despite very different childhoods, they had one thing in common. They were both risk-takers at an early age.

Francia spent much of her childhood with her family in post-World-War-II, war-torn Europe, traveling to different dance schools. When she was twelve, her family moved to London so she could attend the Royal Ballet School, but the school recalled her acceptance once she arrived because they thought she was too tall.

"We had moved there, so it was a terrible situation, but I ended up with a really wonderful teacher. She was a Russian woman, who took me under her wing and became one of the great influences and inspirations in my life," recalled Francia. By the time she turned eighteen she moved to New York and joined the New York City Ballet.

"I was in the company for five years, but at age twenty-three, I felt I had to do something for myself. I really wanted to go to college and, since I had a bad knee injury, I stopped dancing and went to school."

Putting her rising career on hold, she studied art history, literature and political science at NYU and Columbia while working full-time managing an art gallery. She returned to the School of American Ballet as a teacher in 1963.

Meanwhile, Kent grew up in St. George, Utah, the child of a high school basketball coach who did not support his son's artistic aspirations.

"I started taking tap dance when I was eleven, so that was 1951. I was inspired by the films of Fred Astaire. My tap teacher said, 'You should take some ballet. It'll make you a better tap dancer.' In St. George in the early '50s, being a ballet dancer when your father was the coach of the basketball team—that was not easy. It was hardest on my father; he was just humiliated by the whole thing," said Kent. Standing up to his father and society was risky business for a high school kid who wanted to dance, but bowing in to pressure was an even more distasteful option.

Kent studied ballet at the University of Utah's Dance Department and joined the San Francisco Ballet at eighteen years old. The U.S. State Department sponsored cultural exchange programs, so Kent toured with the company in South America, Central America, Africa and the Middle East, meeting many heads of state and other dignitaries and notables. Later, he joined the New York City Ballet, and traveled with the company to Russia, although the Cuban Missile Crisis interrupted their stay. "We were worried we could be bombed by our own country at any second!" he exclaimed.

Francia had already left dancing for college but had agreed to return to the New York Ballet Company as ballet mistress and instructor; she'd realized she loved to teach and to stage productions. She and Kent met in 1962 at a Christmas party, where Francia's flirty sister nabbed Kent for a waltz before he and Francia could do anything more than nod at each other. "I was so mad!" she laughed.

They married, and moved to Indiana in 1969 to have, as they put it, a "normal life"—another risk for two young people who hadn't lived a so-called normal life for many years. Kent got a job at Indiana University as an associate professor, but soon discovered that academia was not his passion.

In 1970, he received another job offer as principal dancer and choreographer of the Bavarian State Opera Ballet in Munich, Germany. The couple debated yet another risky move—this time, with their first child in tow. "I'd staged several ballets in Germany, and I told him, 'I don't want to go. I will go for a year, I'll go anywhere with you for a year, dear, but I don't want to live in Germany.' So we went and we were there for seven years," laughed Francia. "We went with one child and came back with two more," added Kent.

While there, Francia continued to stage ballets for companies around the world, and both she and Kent achieved the elevated status of artistic directors of the Frankfurt Ballet.

In 1977, the pair was persuaded to come to Seattle to run the Pacific Northwest Ballet and School, which was in serious disarray and turned out to be a much more daunting job than they had signed on for.

It took everything Kent and Francia had to juggle the demands of the company and associated ballet school with the demands of raising their young children.

"We somehow believed that we could do this . . . so we rolled up our sleeves and did everything—we painted the walls, cleaned the floors, taught the classes and rehearsed, while Kent choreographed, I staged ballet, and we both went to thousands of meetings trying to persuade people to be interested. *And* we raised three little boys. I mean, we just were like tanks. Somehow, we thought we could do it. If we'd hesitated, everything would have crumbled," said Francia, who cringed as she recalled those challenging years.

Not only did Kent and Francia turn around the small, inadequate dance company and school, but they also single-handedly created the biggest success the company had ever seen, and which quickly became the stuff that legends are made of.

"When we arrived, an out-of-town production of *The Nutcracker* was here," Kent explained, "but we felt *Nutcracker* was so important to every company in the country that we should have our own. Francia is an opera fan, and Houston Opera had done *Magic Flute* with Maurice Sendak as the designer, so she said, 'Well, let's get Maurice Sendak.' Our kids had read his books in German, and so we got his phone number. I called him and went to New York, and we sat down and had lunch. He said 'I'm not the least bit interested in doing *Nutcracker*—'"

"He said, 'I hate ballet,'" added Francia.

"But I talked him into it and we had a great relationship," finished Kent.

Kent and Francia fought tooth and nail for the Stowell/Sendak production to be made; the board of directors felt it would cost too much money and did not immediately give permission to these two risk-takers. In the end, however, they persevered and 1983 saw the first performance of Pacific Northwest Ballet's production of *The Nutcracker*. Since then, it has earned over $100 million and become a Seattle holiday icon, enjoyed by generations.

The risks—large and small—Francia and Kent have taken throughout their lives have paid off, and not just for the two of them. The couple has mentored and nurtured the talent of hundreds of dancers and other people involved in productions, as well as enriched the lives of thousands of ballet enthusiasts.

"Successful self-starters need a lot of great attributes, but for me, two things stand out," explained Kent. "Vulnerability and risk. I always used to think if I wasn't scared, it wouldn't be good. When I was creating a ballet, if I wasn't scared, it wasn't going to come out okay. You have to put yourself on the edge." Francia agreed.

Wise words from a couple who make taking risks look as easy and graceful as a flying leap across the stage.

KEYNOTES

Self-starters take risks—calculated ones, that is. Yes, there are some who take life-threatening risks and live to tell the tale, but for us mere mortals, *measured* risk-taking can get you the results you want—and then some. There are those who never risk and thus stay safe, but how interesting is that? What might you be missing if you don't take a risk?

Ideas to ponder:

1. What does risk-taking mean for you? And where in your life and work are you willing to take a risk?

2. When or where do you take too much risk?

3. Recall a time when you stepped out and took a risk. Was it very rewarding?

Activities:

- Think about several times in the past when you took a risk (either large or small) and you were clearly successful because of it. Write them down. Think of what you can draw from those experiences for the present. What lessons did you learn about yourself and your tolerance for risk? What would you do differently?

- Next time you encounter a particularly risky situation, allow yourself to draw on those previous experiences. Go back to your list and see if what you chose to do during this new, risky situation was on your list of lessons learned.

Eight

Positive Thinking Attracts Possibilities

Positive thinking: Optimistic; affirmative; upbeat; encouraging; confident.

Cynics regularly malign optimists as not being realistic or pragmatic. They view those who see the glass half-full rather than half-empty as dreamers, or even as being irrational. Nothing is further from the truth when it comes to these self-starters. Some have internalized it and made it a habit while others refuse to listen to the negativity.

CREATING YES OUT OF NO

GLORIA BURGESS

Position: Founder/Principal, Jazz, Inc. | **Accomplishment:** Author, poet, keynote speaker; four graduate degrees | **Birthplace:** MS

Gloria Burgess is a study in duality. She is a technology wizard and a poet, a corporate intrapreneur and a small business owner. An academician and a musician. An engineer and an actress.

Gloria's early work history is similar to most young people's—babysitting, bussing tables, working in retail—but that's where the average part of her life ends. Her intelligence and positive attitude, despite a host of negative experiences, provided the momentum for Gloria to reach the top of the career ladder and to start her own successful consulting and executive coaching practice.

Gloria believes in the power of positive thinking. "Self-starters are those who don't take no for an answer. They follow the energy of yes.

They create their own yes when the answers are always no. Self-starters create their own waves, their own wind."

She attributes her positive way of thinking to her father. The first person in his family to go to college, he was her role model for becoming a self-starter. "He kept dreaming out loud and putting it out there that he wanted to go to college. He didn't have a snowball's chance in hell, considering he was a janitor at Ole Miss [University of Mississippi], making $3.50 a day. Since he was well-liked, he was introduced to the author William Faulkner.

"Mr. Faulkner saw something special in my dad and offered to pay for his college education. At first my father refused, saying he didn't want a hand out, but he eventually accepted when Faulkner said, 'This is a gift—no strings attached—but you must pass it on when you're able to.' So, my dad was given a lift when he didn't expect it, and he made the most out of it."

That lift was passed on to Gloria, who earned four graduate degrees in fields as diverse as performance studies, information systems, applied behavioral sciences and leadership, and communication. But not without a few bumps along the way.

"Being born a black female in the '50s was tough. I was told I wasn't good enough—not smart enough, not white enough. My lips didn't look right. Blah, blah, blah," she said calmly. Her professor of education told her she would never make a good teacher; that she'd never amount to anything.

"I heard those comments over and over again. I had a decision to make. I could listen to his garbage, take his vision of me and become a very angry woman, or I could listen to my circle of family and friends and create positive energy around me. I chose to transcend the negative stuff, to say to myself, 'these are lies about you. This is not who you are. This is someone's perception of you. You know who you are, so get over it and keep moving.' That's the path I chose."

Her chosen career path challenged even further the stereotypical notion of a black woman—she opted to pursue technology. "These computer guys didn't know what to do with me. They'd never encountered someone like me—a successful corporate woman, let alone a successful black woman." Gloria figured out a way to succeed, working within huge corporations like Honeywell, Xerox and Citicorp. She carved out a niche for herself where she could innovate, create and invent processes, specifically—user interface designs—that would be good for the organization and customers.

She became so skilled in her field that Aldus, the makers of the design software PageMaker, offered to give Gloria venture capital to start her own digital company.

She did set out on her own in 1994, but instead of a technology company, she started a consulting practice. After thirty years of working for others in the corporate and academic worlds, she knew what her next step would be. "I wanted to become an entrepreneur because I knew that, as an African-American woman, the ceiling wasn't glass, but cement."

Gloria definitely broke through that ceiling. In addition to her coaching and consulting, Gloria has written two books of poetry, a children's book, and a book about her father. Despite the dire predictions of her college professor, she teaches at the University of Washington, the Bainbridge Graduate Institute (Seattle-based MBA programs with emphasis on sustainability), Saybrook Institute (graduate programs based in Seattle), and Leadership Tomorrow (which educates people in non-profits on becoming leaders). She also conceived and developed an innovative leadership educational program for underrepresented K-12 youth and their teachers.

Her love of poetry, music and performing blends together in her work with companies. Whether the goal is excellent customer service, product innovation or outstanding community stewardship, Gloria has reshaped the notion of business as usual. She understands that a leader's most important job is to inspire and encourage, and to offer hope and a sense of possibility. Gloria reminds CEOs and other leaders: you can't inspire others, if you're not inspired.

"More than anything else, conversations that inspire have a net positive impact on productivity and customer care. For those intent on leading thriving organizations, creativity and inspiration feed the soul, providing necessary fuel to cultivate a culture of imagination and innovation," she says.

Her goal remains to assist in developing leadership and learning communities to bridge cultures and support individuals within the workplace.

Gloria has always followed the energy of yes. "I eat this positive philosophy for breakfast, lunch and dinner. That energy moves you forward no matter the obstacles. That energy empowers you to transcend the negativity," she said softly.

GREAT SUCCESS COMES FROM
NEVER GIVING UP

ILONA EUROPA

Position: Founder/CEO, ILONA EUROPA Music & Studio Productions |
Accomplishment: International Billboard-charting singer/songwriter;
songs placed with Sony, Nintendo; selected by Sony Pictures Digital
to be first female included in the company's professional vocal library
series | **Birthplace:** Poland

ILONA EUROPA, a highly acclaimed singer and entrepreneur from
Poland, says, "A self-starter for me is somebody who is not afraid to
look in the mirror and say, 'Okay, today was a hard day. But I still have
a positive belief in myself.'"

Ilona knew from the time she was five that she wanted to be a singer.
"I loved music. That's what I loved to do. I couldn't ever shut up." Her
blue-collar working parents' dream as she grew up in Poland was that
Ilona realize her musical potential. "They always believed in me. They
would say, 'Whatever you want to do, you can do it!'"

Her parents' faith in her inspired her to attend both regular school
and a special music school. "We had no car, so everything was hap-
pening on foot. Every day my mother walked me forty-five minutes

each way to my music lessons, first violin and then later voice, after day school." After high school graduation, she prepared to go into Poland's top music academy.

"But, oops, surprise! I got pregnant and got married instead," she said.

Neither her daughter Marlena's birth nor Ilona's later divorce from her husband slowed her down or derailed her dream. "I had a choice to just be a mom, or to fight again for my place in the music business. I said to myself, 'I know that's what I want to do, so I don't care how long takes me, I just do [sic] anyway!' I positively *knew* I could be successful!" And Ilona did just that. "I wasn't writing my own songs then, but I was recognized as one of the best young singers in Poland." She won singing contest after singing contest, including Poland's version of American Idol, and each time moved one rung higher in the European music hierarchy. "I was sixteen when I started my journey to become a star. I had a positive belief and did the best job I could do."

She soon began recording music. Politics interfered with Ilona's dream in 1981 when the Solidarity movement appeared. This was the first non-communist trade union in Poland and was influential in the ultimate collapse of the Soviet Union. Political repression and martial law ensued as the government attempted to destroy the union. Since no one was allowed outside at night, the Polish entertainment industry was silenced. "We had no place for entertainment because people had trouble to make money [sic] for food and find bread in the stores. We had Army on the streets; we were all so scared."

Despite the difficulty, Ilona never gave up. She knew she would one day succeed. Just months before martial law was declared, Ilona won the top award at a festival for singing patriotic songs, and was chosen to perform for the Polish soldiers. From there, other European contracts emerged. Ilona was the first artist allowed to perform outside Poland during this crisis. Her career was launched.

In this system Ilona was "contracted" out by the Polish arts agency, PAGART. She traveled around the world to critical acclaim, but it wasn't what she wanted. "I was working with a corporation. I wasn't directing my life. They decided where I was to go, what to do." This didn't sit well with a self-starter like Ilona.

A singing contract with an American cruise line changed everything. She fell in love with an American corporate officer who happened to be onboard the day she arrived, and so began a new marriage, a new life in America, a second daughter, Natasha—but no singing career.

After eight years in the U.S., Ilona started in the toughest industry there is—the American music business. This time, it was on her own terms. "I was no longer the cute nineteen-year-old, but in my late thirties, recreating myself in a strange country. But I was unfulfilled. I had many rough moments, many, many tears; a lot of shaking of my hands, saying, 'What now? What to do? What to turn to? No one knows me here and my English is no good.' I really felt I had let myself down because I didn't fulfill who I was, which was a singer, songwriter, musician."

Ilona vowed she would not start at the bottom rung, "doing weddings. I saw success in the end, and I worked on one goal at a time to get there." Ilona refused to be depressed, and instead decided to create momentum towards her goals.

Ilona started by giving voice coaching to young people. Her business accomplished two goals for her: access to new young talent and an opportunity to be known within the music community. She wrote songs for new artists and then produced CDs for them. In 2002, Ilona was selected by Sony to create the world's first vocal sample library for engineers, musicians and deejays titled *ILONA: Universal Female Vocal Toolkit*. This top-selling work gave Ilona a new calling card with producers all around the world, especially those creating pop, electronic and dance music. All of which culminated in record deals and a Billboard charting song, "Live Forever."

Ilona continued recording her own electronic pop songs, which were featured as main songs in games for the Nintendo Wii, Sony PlayStation, and Microsoft Xbox, as well as Abercrombie & Fitch and Adidas stores. She has also been featured on several ABC, CBS, NBC and UPN network affiliate television shows nationwide, and, of course, on global dance radio.

These successes brought Ilona to the attention of Tyra Banks, who chose Ilona's hit "Love in Disguise" as the music for her national promo of America's Next Top Model. Most recently, Ilona produced a song with Grammy winner Michael Bolton for Universal Records in Poland.

Ilona claims her successes were possible because she has always believed she could do it. "I am woman not from this country, I didn't speak English well, but that did not stop me. Whatever fame that comes will give me immense satisfaction. But success for me is what I achieve for myself, what I believed I could become. Nobody will do this for me if I do not do it for myself. I always carry an optimistic vision of myself in my head."

A Positivist Behind the Camera

Dan Geller

Position: President, Geller/Goldfine Productions & Storyline Productions | **Accomplishment:** Winner of more than twenty-one filmmaking awards, including three Emmys | **Birthplace:** Yonkers, NY

Career experts often say the roots to your future career exist in your past—that what you loved to do as a child contains the makings of your vocation as an adult. That is certainly the case with Dan Geller, Emmy Award-winning documentary filmmaker.

When he was a preteen, Dan worked children's birthday parties as a ventriloquist and magician, and made short films and animations. He was further exposed to filmmaking in high school by his father, who had been a teacher and later became a film producer specializing in the adaptation of American literary fiction to the screen.

At Cornell University, Dan worked for a student-run commercial radio station. "That's where I found out I wasn't at all thrilled with working in a corporate structure." Dan was not only on the air, but served as the general manager running the station. "We had a budget of about a half-million dollars a year in 1979 and a staff of over a hundred part-timers and a few full-timers. After just a couple years, I think I knew I wasn't all that turned on about managing a lot of people."

So, after graduation in 1982, he threw away the business graduate school applications he had gathered earlier in the year and signed up for documentary filmmaking instead. Once his Stanford graduate course work was complete, Dan started a corporate video company, creating marketing and training pieces for high-tech companies in Silicon Valley, California.

Conversations around the family dinner table during Dan's growing-up years had prepared him for the frustrations and struggles inherent in his career. "I heard many examples of the hardships and disappointments and paltry earnings that come with any job in its early years, and these conversations helped me keep things in perspective when it was my turn," Dan recalled.

But the biggest lesson his parents instilled in Dan was a belief in the better aspects of humanity—the potential for good in other people. "By nature, I have a hard time staying negative—it's like a ball that wants to float to the surface after being pushed down. I got lucky with my constitution. I have worries, just as we all do, but I work through those worries and also find that exercise or cooking or time with friends and family helps me move on."

During the spare time he eked out between producing corporate videos, he worked on other film projects. These became the initial stages of his full-time documentary filmmaking career.

His creative gifts were recognized in 1989 and his first film, *ISODORA DUNCAN: Movement from the Soul*, with a premiere at the Sundance Film Festival and a Golden Gate Award from the San Francisco International Film Festival.

"The people my partner, Dayna Goldfine, and I feature in our films carry the same characteristic that I believe applies to self-starters—optimism. Optimism about possibilities merges with passion. Optimism creates real fire and excitement about achieving something. It's not a guarantee of success, but you do have the thought that your idea, your project has a reasonable chance of coming to fruition. You're not blindly stupid about it, but whatever you embark upon you view as having a positive outcome, and you accept or embrace that the outcome may differ from what was originally imagined," he said matter-of-factly.

Dan's belief permeates his process for making films. He sets in his mind "the notion that with the right optimistic view and the right amount of effort," he'll make something rewarding to the people featured in the film and those viewing it.

With Dayna Goldfine, his wife as well as his business and creative partner, their synergy infuses their films. "Dayna and I share the belief that the people who fill our movies are those who tend to be fully involved in passionately living out what they are doing. Whether it's college students their freshman year, or a venture capitalist starting without much more than a promise of success, the blend of the two—optimism and passion—comes through," Dan said candidly. "We also have faith that with every movie we make, somehow a meaningful story will unfold with time and it will be of interest to others.

"Our filmmaking is a reinforcing process. I am drawn to stories about people who are facing challenges, some self-made and others by circumstance, but who are trying to make life the most it can be. In doing so, they tend to be positivists. Their optimistic view of the world becomes a feedback loop for me and keeps me in that positive space, too. These people are stimulating to be around, especially when we're making a film that is terribly under-funded and takes years to make."

Dan's career is marked with numerous accomplishments; many awards note his talent. From the Golden Gate award for *ISODORA* to the 1994 Outstanding Directorial Achievement from the Academy of Motion Picture Arts and Sciences for *FROSH: Nine Months in a Freshman Dorm* to *Kids of Survival: The Art & Life of Tim Rollins +K.O.S.*, winner of multiple Emmy Awards in 1999 to *BALLETS RUSSES,* one of the ten best films of 2005, according to *Time Magazine,* the *Los Angeles Times,* the *Hollywood Reporter,* the *San Francisco Chronicle* and *Slate.*

Geller is a hard-core optimist—not surprising, since he threw that business grad school application and its implied promises of financial reward and security in the trash—and nowhere is that more than evident than when he describes his work behind the camera: "There is this wonderful excitement when we can tell a story in a way that is utterly unpredictable and yet you later see it as nothing short of inevitable. That positive approach makes me jump up and down, thinking *yes, yes, YES!*"

Transforming Lives, Thanks to a Fair Start

Megan Karch

Position: Executive Director, FareStart | **Accomplishment:** Named one of *Puget Sound Business Journal's* "Top 20 Women of Influence" in 2007 | **Birthplace:** Cleveland, OH

"I see people at their best every single day at FareStart," said Megan Karch, executive director of the social entrepreneurial organization dedicated to transforming the lives of homeless men and women in Seattle.

"We're all about positivity: Whether it's our students wanting to change their lives—which is just an incredible experience to watch—or our donors who want to give back, or our volunteers who want to help, or our staff who have committed to changing others' lives. I mean, how can you *not* love it?" she said fervently.

Megan and FareStart are a perfect fit. Megan's optimistic approach to life and entrepreneurial savvy are reflected in the organization she heads, which gives people a way back from homelessness and dire circumstances.

Megan's organization has transformed the lives of over 3,500 people as it provides culinary job training and placement. More importantly, students in the program prepare meals—over four million since 2000—for other disadvantaged men, women and children in the community. By helping others, these men and women gain valuable skills and experience in food service. "More than 80 percent of our program graduates," Megan said proudly, "secure living-wage employment in the food service and hospitality industry."

For Megan, optimism has always been a key driver in her life. "I look at opportunities in a positive way; I just don't dwell on the negative stuff. Without positive thinking, I would have too many reasons not to do something."

Growing up on a farm east of Cleveland, Megan learned a life lesson during high school from her father, a corporate attorney. "I hated the tedium of the job I had packaging food products in a plant and complained about it often. One night over dinner, I said to my dad, 'How do you work every day and not just look at the clock constantly? Is this what life *is*?' I was pretty horrified at the thought.

"My dad said to me, 'You know, Megan, I look at the clock too, but for a different reason. I look at the clock to see how much more work I can do before I need to go home. You should always do what you love.'"

Her father's advice helped her to view the world with a glass-half-full philosophy, especially as she has built FareStart into one of the most successful non-profit programs in Seattle.

Megan has always known she loves helping people. During college, she worked as a summer camp counselor, and upon graduation she secured a position as a vocational counselor for Humanim in Columbia, MD. There she found her purpose, working as a job coach helping those with mental illness. "That was my first real job, and I loved it because it was about having people look at the here and now and not the past. It was about, 'So, okay, you've been dealt a pretty tough deck; now what do we do about it?'"

The non-profit was just in its infancy at the time. "It was fabulous. As it grew, I grew with it. I ended up finding opportunity after opportunity after opportunity."

After thirteen years, Megan was ready to spread her wings and fly west. She landed her current position with FareStart in 2000.

Megan is a classic intrapreneur—someone who starts programs, projects, services and initiatives within an organization. "I always want more. I want to build new programs or expand existing ones." And so she has, including a barista program for runaways and street youth. She bought and remodeled a building so she could start a FareStart restaurant, with local chefs mentoring her students in the kitchen.

Her positive energy permeates the building. "When you're working with people who have a mental illness or are homeless or disabled, and they have seen their dreams dashed and their futures unfulfilled, you have to be an optimist," she said.

Her positive thinking works. According to Megan, "Enrollment in our programs has increased by fifty percent in the past two years!"

She often repeats how wonderful or how fabulous her work has been—how much she enjoys it. Despite the life-changing impact her work has had on the homeless community, Megan truly believes she is the fortunate one.

"I just take our students where they are right now. Their plans have been destroyed. So it's always, 'Well, what do we do now? How do we rebuild?' How do we take someone who was abused or a former prison inmate—someone with no home, no family and all things of material value taken from them—and try to restore human dignity? Well, we do! We empower people to transform their lives every day; we remove the dark cloud that hovered over their heads. We give them a fair start."

It all starts with positive thinking.

Never Say Never

Ginny Ruffner

Position: Artist | **Accomplishment:** Recognized worldwide as a preeminent artist, glass blower, painter, sculptor | **Home:** Seattle, WA

Five weeks, five months, five years. That's the amount of time Ginny Ruffner spent in a coma, in a hospital and in a wheelchair after a car accident in North Carolina almost ended her life in 1991.

Today, Ginny is an internationally celebrated glass artist. Meet her, and her strong determination and optimistic approach to life are immediately apparent within her diminutive frame.

She brushes off the accident and recovery ordeal as a "non-event," but it was truly her character, doggedness and positive thinking that pulled her through. "I'm a lemonade-from-lemons kind of person," she said. "My glass is never less than half full."

After the accident, Ginny couldn't talk or walk. She had double-vision and had lost the use of her left hand. "I was an aerobics instructor, yet I couldn't move. I couldn't even make a sound for months. Thank God I wasn't an opera singer," she laughed.

Her recovery amazed the specialists. Doctors frequently warned her she wouldn't be able to do something and she always responded, "You just watch me!"

Ginny laughed, "I was like a three-year-old who wouldn't cooperate unless she was told she couldn't do it. In my mind, I had to learn to talk so I could tell them to drop dead!

"It's a good thing I like challenges," she added.

Ginny's positive attitude is a byproduct, or perhaps the cause, of her career as an artist. "The can-do attitude, the willingness to make a fool of yourself—it's part of art. You have to be willing to try stuff, to be embarrassed in order to express your art. This attitude works no matter what kind of a self-starter you are," she explained.

She called upon her strong determination to heal herself after her accident. "I remember I had bought this lovely house, and I kept banging my wheelchair into the walls. I thought, 'No way.' So less than two weeks after I moved in, I decided, 'Okay, I'll walk, and that's it.'"

Along with her positive attitude, Ginny has had artistic aspirations since she was a child. As a young person growing up in a small town in South Carolina, Ginny always painted and drew. In high school she taught art lessons to neighborhood kids and majored in painting and drawing at University of Georgia.

She said her family background was a large part of what made her a self-starter. "My parents were always very supportive. After I graduated college in 1974, they encouraged me to go to law school, since I was so contentious. I took the LSAT and realized it wasn't for me. So my parents said, 'Okay, we'll pay for graduate school but you have to take shorthand as a backup,'" she laughed.

While in graduate school she learned on her own how to drill and cut glass, techniques that would later serve her well. "I decided I needed more light in my paintings, so I wanted to learn even more about glass. At the time nobody knew diddly about it."

Scant books, tools or techniques existed for her to learn lampworking—a technique she observed at fairs where men were making little glass animals. It involves manipulating the glass with a tool or by using gravity. "I knew there had to be more to this art than glass swans and ships associated with cotton candy and corn dogs!"

Her strong interest led to a six-year apprenticeship in lampworking. She adapted the technique used to make scientific tools so she could create ribbons and panes of glass and to enlarge the scale of her work. "In order to teach, I had to buy all the equipment. Since there were no pre-made tools, I had them handmade and then used them when I taught at various craft schools.

"If you can believe it, today they have lampworking societies, conferences and a bazillion companies who sell tools for this. There was nothing when I started," she chuckled.

After six years perfecting her craft, she was asked in 1984 to teach lampworking at the famed Pilchuck School of Glass in Washington state. As her talent was recognized, her art began to be shown around the country and internationally. Countries like Switzerland, Germany, France, Japan, China, Australia and Italy were all enthralled.

Ginny's immensely creative art is known for its thought-provoking images created with intelligence and inspiration. She has expanded her artistic repertoire beyond canvas and glass, and now works in metal as well.

Art isn't Ginny's only passion. Always a bookworm, she finds written words inspiring. "Reading is extremely thought-provoking. Think about the twenty-six squiggles that make up the alphabet of our language. Depending on the way you order them and put those clumps together, you can convey anything."

These days, Ginny reads scientific books to learn more about the brain, which translates into her art. "I find this stuff sends me into gales of wonderment. During the act of reading, words start out as visual, then the brain decodes them, either verbally, written or artistically. There are all those levels of transformation, all those levels of thinking that go into art."

It's no wonder Ginny finds the brain so fascinating—her work is inspired and driven by her curiosity and wonder about the world around her. "I say that thinking is one thing that has made me a success.

I'm analyzing, thinking . . . thinking informs my work. It helps me understand the validity of risk-taking or the absurdity of not going ahead and making a fool of yourself. You just have to move forward with hopeful intent."

Her work is featured in solo and group shows across the United States and around the world and has become part of museum exhibitions and collections in such prestigious places as The Louvre, The Smithsonian, Carnegie Museum of Art and The American Craft Museum, to name a few. She has been featured on National Public Radio (NPR) and in hundreds of books and articles. She also lectures and teaches and has received untold honors for her work. An acclaimed documentary was made in 2010 of her art.

Ginny continues to stretch herself, personally and professionally. True to her creative and playful spirit, she is still "trying stuff." With her ingrained positive attitude, she'll not only decorate her more-than-half-full glass, she'll also highlight its adaptive functions, intrinsic value, unique qualities and universal appeal. Much like the woman herself.

KEYNOTES

Self-starters are optimistic. Not sunny, Pollyanna types, but believers in positive thinking, knowing it will result in positive outcomes. Some people seem to be born with a proclivity toward seeing the best in situations and people. Others of us are brooding types, whose negative thoughts fester, compound and become larger than originally imagined.

Nearly every self-starter in this book mentioned positive thinking as an important trait. Or if they didn't, they naturally exuded it. Studies have shown that viewing the world with the glass half-full approach makes for a happier, more joyful person. When you make mental tick marks of those negative people with whom you work, do you think they get less done or give up sooner? Are they offered fewer opportunities? Do they block creative thoughts? Are they afraid to take risks? Or do they have less passion?

Think about these questions:

1. If you're not naturally inclined to thinking positively, how can you make positive thinking work for you?

2. What three positive statements could you make about yourself?

3. What positive affirmations are you already saying to yourself?

4. Do you have a set schedule when you say these positive statements? Or is there something that triggers you to do this? When are other times you could use these positive statements?

Activities:

- When that internal critic starts beating you up and you can't stop the negative thoughts, make it a habit to leave the physical space you're in. Get up and go to a different venue: Move to a different room. Go get a drink of water. Walk around the block. Take your laptop and work at a coffee shop or some other place where you're typically productive. Once there, engage in a different activity that frees your mind or assists you in working through the problem in an analytical rather than emotional way.

- Write down positive affirmations, which are, essentially, statements about yourself in a positive light. For example, *I always figure out the best or most logical or most empathic approach to a problem.* Say these statements each day.

- Thought leaders in the human potential movement offer workshops, books, CDs, etc., to assist. Two are featured in this book. Go online and explore their offerings and those of other experts whose wise words resonate with you.

NINE

COMPASSION ENRICHES SUCCESS

Compassion: Feeling; humanity; mercy; charity; to commiserate; empathy; consideration.

All the self-starters interviewed held the firm belief that reaching out to help communities—regionally, nationally or globally—is part of the price and the joy of being a human being. Some self-starters pursued their conviction through their own organizations; others donated time, talent and treasure to causes they knew would support humankind.

THE MEMORY MAVEN

ROBERTA DIAZ BRINTON

Position: Professor of Pharmacology, Endowed Chair in Therapeutic Discovery and Development, University of Southern California | **Accomplishment:** Discovered strategies to prevent Alzheimer's disease in women | **Birthplace:** NJ

Crowned "the memory maven" by *U.S. News and World Report* in 2004, what Dr. Roberta Diaz Brinton discovered is both revolutionary and mind-boggling: a brain-selective hormone therapy for women to prevent Alzheimer's disease (AD).

Millions of boomers who are facing their own sinking estrogen levels now have a crusader in their corner. "Alzheimer's is ravaging our nation, and this devastation will grow exponentially as baby boomers age. Sixty-eight percent of those diagnosed with AD are women. These women are being taken away, bit by bit. I just had to find out why," Roberta said ardently.

This "can-do, will-do, and have-to-do" family ethos propelled her to amazing accomplishments.

Roberta came from a working-class family in New Jersey. Since college was not financially feasible, she enrolled at a lab tech school in 1969 where a series of "transformative experiences," as she calls them, began to shape her life and career.

The first was her night job at a mental institution. "It was really quite Draconian. I worked in a tiny basement lab with a naked bulb hanging from the ceiling. I was eighteen years old. One night, I went into the women's ward to collect specimens. The women crowded around me, touching me, desperate for affection, for the human touch, for a human connection. That poignant memory still resonates," Roberta said tenderly.

Roberta believes her life's work has been 'divinely guided.' "God has always opened doors for me and then had the good sense to boot me through them," she laughed.

Her door opened in an Arizona laboratory where she worked as a lab tech in an academic pediatric clinic. "I had always lived within a hierarchy—in church there were certain pews you sat in, in society there was a certain strata, in marriage there was a hierarchal role to be filled, in jobs there was a hierarchy of those with titles and those without," said Roberta.

But in the lab, Roberta explained, there was "a wonderful team of healers. No hierarchy existed, just a distribution of gifts and talents. My job was to teach medical students laboratory procedures and how to interpret lab results." There, Roberta experienced a transforming moment—an epiphany—that she was just as smart as the medical students. And so, with encouragement, she began college at twenty-five.

Two years later, in 1979, she graduated Phi Beta Kappa from the University of Arizona, then went on to graduate school, and in less than five years she had her PhD.

For twenty-five years Roberta persevered, working non-stop toward the goal of discovering therapies that can prevent and treat Alzheimer's. Her work has been filled with ups and downs—the constant challenge to generate research funding (even though she had made this astounding discovery, she had to wait eight years for funding), along with a divorce, grueling hours—but the goal, the commitment to others to find a cure, sustained her.

She remains driven by the knowledge that "if no effective preventive therapeutics are developed, within forty-two years, one in forty-five Americans will be afflicted with Alzheimer's."

Another one of Dr. Brinton's dreams was to advance the interest of science in schools. After she joined the University of Southern California (USC) pharmacology department, she was able to "actualize her dream," as she put it. Thus, for the past twenty-two years, she has volunteered her time as the director of the USC's STAR (Science, Technology and Research) program. STAR provides opportunities for minority and low-income high school students to "learn science by conducting real science that really matters," Roberta explained, by joining a USC research team and working with college students and researchers. The high schoolers get actual lab experience; one of those labs is that of her husband, who is developing neural prosthetics for the brain to replace damaged memory circuits.

Thanks to Roberta and others committed to STAR, 100 percent of the STAR students attend top-tier research universities and liberal arts colleges. Eighty-one percent go on to graduate school in medicine or other sciences.

"As I tell the STAR students, 'If you want to change the world, become a scientist. Scientists are those individuals whose brains see beyond the unseen to what could be, and who then begin the long, arduous and exciting journey from hypothesis to discovery.'"

Brinton has published more than 100 scientific reports and serves on advisory boards for the National Institute of Mental Health, the Alzheimer Drug Discovery Foundation and the Society for Neuroscience. She is also co-founder of a biotechnology company and a patent holder for several therapeutics.

Brinton is keenly aware of the ticking of the biological clock to prevent Alzheimer's disease in menopausal women, who are most affected. She is confident that she and her colleagues will beat the clock for the baby boomer women, their daughters and grandchildren to come so that they will all live the full measure of their life—and remember it.

Fighting a Global Problem Close to Home

Jared Greenberg

Position: Consultant; Co-Founder, Somaly Mam Foundation |
Accomplishment: Raised $2 million to combat human trafficking |
Birthplace: NJ

As twenty-seven-year-old Jared Greenberg ticks off the astounding statistics, his voice is emotional and urgent.

"Human trafficking is the second-largest organized crime in the world. It has become a bigger business than drugs. Children as young as five are sold into sexual slavery for as little as $10. Each year, one million children are exploited into the global commercial industry of sexual slavery. Two to four million women and children are sold into prostitution every twelve months."

When he was twenty-two years old and a newly hired grad, Jared took on these alarming statistics and created a foundation to heal the victims. Though his adult life is nothing short of amazing, Jared's early life was pretty normal. He grew up in a middle-class family in New

Jersey, and after high school went into the Air Force Academy. Jared completed his undergrad studies, served thirteen months as an officer, and left the Air Force to join a management consulting company.

Then it got interesting.

Jared saw a documentary on sexual slavery. "It just blew my mind that this was going on today. It's going on in our backyards, and young girls are being forced to have sex with whoever is paying. It really pissed me off more than anything."

This problem haunted him for two years. He talked about it at work; he mentioned it in social situations. "I'd bring it up at cocktail parties or with my friends, complaining, 'Why doesn't someone do something about this? Why don't the politicians do anything? Aren't there some super wealthy people that could help out!?'"

He always answered his own questions with, "Well, one day, when I'm older. Well, one day, when I'm richer. Well, one day when I have more connections, then I'll actually go ahead and do something."

He recalled, "I got sick of hearing myself talk about how, when circumstances became perfect, I'd do something about it. Then I woke up one day and realized if I'm not willing to do anything about it now, why would anyone else?"

So Jared got together for sushi and sake with his friend Nick Lumpp and hatched an idea, one that took on a life of its own. "We had a little too much sake, and I said to Nick, 'I'm done complaining. I'm going to raise a million dollars to combat sexual slavery and I'm going to do it within a year.'"

Jared is the first to admit his task seemed impossible. He had no background in fundraising, nor did he come from wealth and connections. "After another drink, my friend joined me and we both committed to it. Because we knew we could really impact the lives of these young girls whose freedom had been completely taken away from them. They're being ignored by the world."

Then the research began—nights and weekends devoted to finding out as much as they could about human trafficking. "We had made this crazy commitment and weren't sure how we were gonna do it." Their Internet search brought up information about a woman in

Cambodia, Somaly Mam, a former victim who spent her time reha- bilitating girls she'd helped to rescue from the brothels, and provide a safe haven for them.

So they maxed their credit cards and took two weeks' vacation—much to the chagrin of their families and bosses—and flew to Cambodia. "They thought we were pretty crazy, not having any idea what we were gonna do." But Jared and Nick believed that to raise money and honor their commitment, they had to see with their own eyes what was going on.

Somaly showed them the shelters and took them undercover into the brothels. "Once you see it firsthand, it changes you. Seeing a documentary was one thing, but all of sudden you meet a six-year-old girl in the shelter who was a sex slave and was tortured. You can't even imagine or comprehend it."

Somaly shared her dream with them: to create a U.S.-based founda- tion, using her name to get the word out to the rest of the world and eventually work in other countries.

Now the pressure was on. They had agreed to help Somaly but faced a big challenge. "We had no idea how to do it. Maybe that was our biggest advantage—not knowing how, we could break every rule in the book."

Jared did anything and everything necessary to see his pledge through. "You see," said Jared, "I believe self-starters make commitments greater than themselves. They make a stand for something. They speak about it with passion. I think any single person can do that. It doesn't take any special skill or ability, other than to not get discouraged by all the circumstances you face. And it helps if you're pissed off. It's what really kept us going; that's when good change happens."

The next challenge was to have an event to raise money and increase awareness of this global problem. "We needed to have a fundraiser. So where would be a good place to have it? We thought, 'Well, how about the United Nations?!'"

Through networking, they met people who landed them on the Tyra Banks television show, which then led to an article in the *New York Times*. "We were very, very lucky with all the media coverage that we received. It added credibility to our foundation."

Throughout their whirlwind beginning, the Somaly Mam Foundation faced many challenges, such as not having the requisite eight months to be considered a charity. The upshot? "Our charity application was fast-tracked. The night of the event it was a packed house, even with some celebrity showings." The climax to the evening was that they had surpassed their original goal and raised not one but two million dollars during the year 2007.

Since then, the foundation has received press in *USA Today*, the *Denver Post, Fox News*, and is featured in every Body Shop retail store across North America. The Somaly Mam Foundation now has a board of directors with such luminaries as actresses Darryl Hannah and Susan Sarandon.

Jared is proud of his success and hopes others will follow their own passion for compassion. "The attitude I hope a lot of people have is you have to take a stand for something, make a commitment to it. You don't know how you're going to accomplish it but you figure it out along the way. And you don't get discouraged by the circumstances. You go forward anyway. It's just very necessary."

HE LEAPS TO HELP LATINO STUDENTS

RICARDO SANCHEZ

Position: Founder, Latino/a Educational Achievement Project (LEAP) |
Accomplishment: Founded non-profit organization to improve academic
achievement of Latino students; successfully advocated for new law
allowing undocumented students to pay in-state tuition for college |
Birthplace: MT

Ricardo Sanchez sat ramrod straight around a table with his peers at El Centro de la Raza, a well-known multi-service organization that advocates for Latinos in Seattle, Washington.

Latino educators were discussing the academic trends for Latino students and weren't satisfied with how "the system" was addressing the needs of the state's fastest growing student population. Ricardo remembered saying to them, "You know what? We *can't* wait for Bill Gates or anyone else to come to the rescue. So let's get going." And they did.

The "us" Ricardo spoke about is young Latinos and Latinas whose educational outlook is dire.

Scary statistics kicked Ricardo into high gear in 1996, as the director of communications for the Office of Superintendent of Public

Instruction in Washington State. With access to the data, he learned the truth: Latino children scored the lowest of any ethnic group in reading, language arts, math and science at virtually all grade levels. "I said to myself that we could either assume that our kids are less intelligent than everybody else's and just throw in the towel, or we could do something about it," Ricardo said.

Two years later, having gathered support from Latino leaders and other concerned educators, he started the Latino/a Educational Achievement Project (LEAP). This organization became the pinnacle of Ricardo's activism, and helped fulfill his desire to do something substantial for Latino students.

In Billings, Montana, Rick (his childhood nickname) grew up on what some would consider "the right side of the tracks." As the only Latino family in a white neighborhood, his parents were determined that they would live in a safe neighborhood. "None of us were rich; we had a one-bedroom house and seven kids. We wouldn't even have had a car or a television if my older sister had not started working full-time while in high school."

The beginning of Rick's evolution into Ricardo—a very visible and purposeful acknowledgment of his heritage—began after college graduation, when he secured a job with the YMCA in Washington State. He discovered his true path, which was to be of service to others and to be good at it. Ricardo, it turned out, was a self-starter.

"For me, in the non-profit world, a self-starter is someone with a mindset and a willingness to work hard for a cause. You want to *do* something. You want the satisfaction of knowing that you've improved a condition or a life; you've addressed something that's wrong in the system," he said passionately.

Each job Ricardo held added to his reputation and affirmed his self-starter attributes. To become better known, he began a Chicano basketball league and started listening to the concerns of the Latino community. To learn more about public policy and community organizing, he worked briefly for the Seattle City Council and the City's Office of Management and Budget. "That's where the action was. That's where it all happens in city government," he said.

By the early '80s, with budgeting experience under his belt, he became executive director of *Concilio for the Spanish Speaking*, a council of various Latino organizations. "When they hired me, I was as green as an evergreen tree. But I wanted it badly because this job fulfilled my two needs. The first was to become deeply involved in the Latino community. The second was to make my background part of my identity. That's the year I officially changed my name from Rick to Ricardo."

Then he jumped into the thick of it. "At the *Concilio*, one of my first advocacy roles was to get more Latinos hired by the City of Seattle, where we were only marginally represented. We didn't like being excluded." Ricardo exposed discrepancies in city hiring, and his work got the attention of the mayor and the media. In the early '80s, he was quoted in *The Seattle Times* as referring to one large city department as "a snake pit of discrimination." As a result of a series of meetings, "changes were made in hiring practices," said Ricardo, "and Latinos started showing up on the employment lists."

His next job, as the director of communications with the state's Office of Superintendent of Public Instruction, was the final rung on his government-career ladder. "I was privy to all the test scores in the state and I noticed a tragic trend. Something was very wrong with how we educated our Latino children," he lamented. In 1998, he founded LEAP in order to address the issues. Twelve years later, LEAP has made progress and has helped make a difference in students' lives.

Several school districts, colleges and universities now partner with LEAP to carry out its mission. Another sign of progress is a yearly education conference at which more than 600 students from across the state attend. While at the conference, students are encouraged to excel academically and to become leaders in their schools and communities.

Taking students to the state capitol in Olympia to help them understand government and how they can be part of the civic process is one important part of the annual conference. "Oftentimes students leave the conference feeling empowered and motivated to stay in school, now envisioning themselves as future legislators," Sanchez said.

Additionally, LEAP identifies important public educational policies that can help Latino students improve academically. In 2002 and

2003, LEAP was the main force behind a legislative proposal to allow undocumented students to pay resident tuition to attend college. In 2003, the House Bill (HB 1079) was approved by the legislature.

"For me, it's really about a sense of fair play; using public policy to right injustices, to address something wrong in the system—that has always been my mindset," said Ricardo.

"In the case of HB 1079, young children, some at infancy, are brought to the U.S. and then educated entirely in our system. They did nothing but obey their parents in coming here. Why should we punish them, especially young scholars with 3.5 or higher GPAs, by making it impossible for them to attend college?" he asked.

Due to passage of House Bill 1079 (HB 1079) in 2003, more than 2,500 students have qualified to pay the in-state tuition rate at public colleges and universities in Washington. One young woman, a student from a farm-worker family in eastern Washington that LEAP helped with scholarship assistance, has earned a law degree from the University of Washington.

"For me this journey has been about issues of justice and human dignity. I'm willing to work with and through the system to get things changed. That's what made me a self-starter."

GIVING HIS THIRD EIGHT TO HELP THE HURTING

PHIL M. SMART, SENIOR

Position: Chair, Phil Smart Mercedes Benz | **Accomplishment:** Seattle's First Citizen; Santa Claus for forty-seven years to 6,541 patients at Seattle's Children's Hospital | **Birthplace:** WA

"Santa, am I going to die?" Phil Smart has been asked that question a thousand times in his forty-seven years bedside at Seattle's Children's Hospital and Regional Medical Center. At ninety years old, Phil has looked into the eyes of 6,541 sick and dying children as the hospital's first evening-ward male volunteer and yearly Santa Claus.

To Phil, there is nothing greater than giving a piece of himself to help those who need him. "If you give yourself away to others, you will achieve all your dreams. The giving away causes you to be involved in others' lives; customers' lives, peers' lives—those in need. To be a self-starter you have to decide what you're going to do with your God-given talents, whether it's to self-start a company or a cause, or follow a dream."

Phil has spoken to over 650 organizations in ten states and in Europe about community service and lessons learned from sick and dying children, all for gratis. It's part of Phil's ethos of giving back.

This philosophy was solidified when Phil was a Boy Scout. He recalled, "It came to me from Boy Scouting, eighty-one years ago when I took the Boy Scout oath, 'On my honor . . .' The twelve points of law—they go together like my two hands clasped together, and, for me, it changed my life. When people would say to me, 'Well, you Scouting guys run around in short pants and help old ladies cross the street,' I would say, 'Yeah, that's what we do. But we do more.'"

Phil grew up during the Depression and started working when he was seven years old—selling the *Saturday Evening Post* door to door for five cents a copy. "That's when I was initiated into the sales business. I learned about accounts receivable because people didn't always pay me. I also learned about customer service."

Phil claims he can sell anything as long as it doesn't melt. He has sold straw hats, cement, dry cleaning solutions, clothes hangers, washers, dryers, plumbing supplies and cars. "I swear to you I came out of the womb with this selling gene. There's a picture of me at six months giving a thumbs-up as I sit on my mother's lap," he smiled.

World War II interrupted his plans to attend the University of Washington, and Phil was shipped over to French Morocco with General George Patton. "My company hauled infantry into the line as we fought Erwin Rommel, the desert fox," Phil says. He was awarded the Soldier's Medal for saving a crewmember from a bomber that was about to explode, and left the Army Air Corps as a colonel.

Phil Smart started selling cars in 1952 and opened Phil Smart Mercedes Benz in 1959. For the first twenty-five years in business, his dealership was the only Mercedes dealership in Seattle.

Phil Smart's very successful career in cars has allowed him to volunteer in the community. "I discovered decades ago that there are eight hours of societal pain during which I can self-start. What I mean by this is that you have eight hours to sleep, eight hours to work and then another eight hours to give away to the hurt, the hungry, the homeless, the unemployed, the old, the illiterate and the addict. It's the 'third eight' that defines the quality of people's lives," said Phil.

He decided to focus on the people in the "hurt" category of his social pain list and started his long record of volunteering at Children's Hospital. He decided he needed to do more, so he volunteered to play Santa on Christmas Day and has done so for the past twenty-eight years. He has written a book about his experiences and created a DVD. Proceeds from both go to the hospital.

"Self-starting is dramatically important. It will force you to get out of bed, get off the davenport and do it. You can't wait for anyone to give you permission or tell you what to do. You follow your dreams and goals. You never compromise, you just do it; *then* it becomes a habit. It starts in your head and then your heart turns on, and there's no limit," said Phil reverentially.

"What happens when you give yourself away?" he asked. "You become involved in other people's lives and it changes your life. Why? Because God has allowed us twenty-four hours with ups and downs, ins and outs, and that's the way it is. And I'm still wanting those next twenty-four-hours!" said Phil.

Phil is still giving this 'third eight' to the community and has no plans to stop. His commitment to volunteering exemplifies his belief in more tomorrows. "I've warned my receptionist that someday she will receive a long, long, long distance phone call. She'll ask the caller, 'With whom would you like to speak? Phil Senior or Phil Junior?'

"The caller will say, 'I want to speak with the old one.'

"My receptionist will respond, 'I don't mean to be forward but may I tell him who is calling?'

"The voice will say, 'This is God calling.'

"'Pardon me? This is God calling and you want to speak to Phil Senior?'

"'Yes, please. Is he in?'

"'Well, I don't mean to be rude or abrupt, but he told me to tell you if I should get a call like this, I should put you on hold because he isn't through yet.'"

CREATING GOODWILL AROUND THE GLOBE

BOB WALSH

Position: CEO, One World 2011 | **Accomplishment:** Goodwill Games; professional basketball's March Madness; facilitated hundreds of millions of dollars in investments in former Soviet countries | **Birthplace:** MA

"My parents brought me up to care about other people. It's possible they went overboard," said Bob dryly. After reading even a partial list of Bob's accomplishments in the past twenty-five years, it's obvious this is a gross understatement—fortunately for the millions of people around the world who have benefitted from his selflessness.

Bob Walsh is a compassionate man. "There are a lot of people who have done a lot to stay in 'safe territory.' Maybe they're smarter than I am, but they don't step up because their ideas are not big enough, or they're not challenging enough, so they're not really risking much," he said forcefully.

Quick! Name a few famous people you would like to meet. If they were alive during the past few decades, more likely than not, Bob knows them. He's met such varied personalities as former NBA star Bill Russell; former President of the Republic of Georgia, Eduard Shevardnadze; CNN's Ted Turner; business tycoon Armand Hammer; Jordan's Queen Raina; 1960s black nationalist, Malcolm X; Minister of the Nation of Islam, Louis Farrakhan; and psychologist and LSD advocate, Timothy Leary. Bob Walsh knows them all.

At some point, he's approached these and many others to ask for their help to right a wrong, to expose an evil, to make the world a better place. Those sound like high-flying words for just one man but keep in mind he's been labeled everything from brilliant businessman, entrepreneur and innovative genius to dreamer extraordinaire and humanitarian.

Bob grew up outside of Boston, the second child of two successful parents; his mother ran five newspapers in the '50s and his father was a journalist. After college, he got the media bug and joined a television station while simultaneously working as a program director for a radio station.

Bob's strong sense of right and wrong sometimes put him in harm's way. In the 1960s, he interviewed controversial figures like Timothy Leary and the Ku Klux Klan imperial wizard. Why? "Because I was doing the right thing by exposing their extremist views. And the right thing is that people shouldn't be prejudiced. People shouldn't hurt people."

Why does he do this? Why does he throw himself into risky projects that could blow up in his face? "If you noticed that something needed doing, but you didn't believe you should be the one to take it on, or if you didn't take a risk to make it happen, where have you been? What have you done?" Bob asked rhetorically.

"The self-starter knows the answer to these questions," he continued. "Self-starters can't just sit by and watch a giant, critical need go unfulfilled; they will act on it."

Bob's motivation continues to put people together to build relationships and make the world a better place. He not only acts on this drive but he'll rally people around the world and from the highest echelons of industry, entertainment, sports, politics and non-profits to lend their skills and stature to the cause.

In 1985, because of Bob's excellent reputation to pull off events with staggering success—think of the NBA's "March Madness," a media event solely attributed to Bob—he received a phone call from CNN's Ted Turner. The U.S. boycott of the 1980 Olympics in Moscow and the Soviet's boycott of the 1984 Los Angeles Olympics sparked Ted's idea for the Goodwill Games, which were designed to foster better relations between the U.S. and the then-Soviet Union. Turner was ready to provide financing and he asked Bob to take on the huge project.

They set a 1986 date for the first Goodwill Games, slated for Moscow, and a 1990 date for the U.S.'s counterpart event, to be held in Seattle. For the next four years, Bob spent 70 percent of his time in Russia. "I was called a 'communist lover' by the press. The papers went after me. It was terrible; it was not easy," Bob recalled. He worked his magic, the door to Russia was opened, and he quickly built relationships with the Russians. When the 1988 Armenian earthquake rocked that corner of the Soviet Union, Bob worked with Mikhail Gorbachev, former head of state, to bring in medical equipment and personnel. "Yeah, we saved a bunch of lives then," Bob smiled. He also organized flights out of Russia to the United States for seriously ill children needing bone marrow transplants and open-heart surgeries. "Back then, we still considered Russia 'the evil empire,' and they thought we were all CIA agents, so this was tough going," he chuckled.

Bob's hard work on the Goodwill Games yielded tremendous results. Thanks to the relationships and trust he had established, Bob brought 3,000 Russian athletes, the Bolshoi Ballet, the Russian Symphony, the Russian Opera and 43 other major art and cultural events to Seattle in 1990. He also organized people-to-people home stays.

"I believed, like Ted, that it was the right thing to do to bring the Soviets over here," he emphasized. Over 53,000 people met and talked with the Russians during the 1990 Goodwill Games alone. "People don't realize the effect bringing people together can have." Thousands of Soviets connected with thousands of Americans. Not only that, but one billion dollars from a variety of sources was invested in the state of Washington as part of bringing the games to fruition.

Bob's newest vision is to bring the Muslim world to Seattle, focusing specifically on women and youth. The event, called One World 2011, will be four months long and start in 2011 on the tenth anniversary of 9/11. "I've risked everything—my house, my health, my future. It does get lonely," he admitted when prodded. "I'm sixty-nine years old and a single father with a sixteen-year-old."

Because of his dedication to bringing people from around the world together in peace, then-President Shevardnadze presented Bob in 2002 with the highest award ever given to a foreigner: he was named an 'Honorary Citizen of Georgia.' Bob has also received the Supreme Soviet Award from then-President Gorbachev; he also received the Martin Luther King, Jr., Award and other special recognition from Presidents Ronald Reagan and George H. W. Bush. Also of note, the global humanitarian organization CARE credits him for getting them in the door to the former Soviet Union.

"You've gotta do what you gotta do. You just can't give up on what you believe in," Bob insisted. "Everything I've done, I believe, is the right thing to do. For me, it's about the relationships and helping people.

"I've just taken a different road than other people have." Around the globe and close to home, Bob's abundant compassion compels him to travel that road and bring people together—despite overseas dangers and risks on the home front, too. As he says, what's the worst thing that can happen? From what we've seen, not much that's bad, but definitely a whole lot of good.

KeyNotes

Self-starters lose themselves in people. They become involved in charitable causes and give of their time and talent to issues they feel passionate about. Others know their work will change lives, make a better world, save lives. These qualities were never more evident than among the people profiled in this chapter.

Our featured self-starters also realized that when they selflessly gave of themselves, they were rewarded many times over—and often unexpectedly. Sometimes the benefits of their compassionate efforts were as simple and uncomplicated as a heartfelt thank-you or a smile from a sick or starving child. Other times, our self-starters received more tangible evidence of their efforts: increased business, an award or recognition, an opportunity.

Ask yourself:

1. What are the basic principles of my life? What do I value?

2. How much do I let my world preoccupy myself and don't look up and out?

3. What pulls at my heartstrings? Evaluate that as a place to serve others.

Activities:

- Determine what abilities/talent/gifts you have to serve in ways you identified above.

- Determine where you might put those gifts to use in a caring and compassionate way for others.

- Keep a personal journal about how you feel when you have freely given of yourself using a talent.

- Don't measure the results of your selfless acts, but when something positive happens to you because of them, make a note of it and read it later, when you're tired or exhausted or focusing too much on your own problems.

- Keep on giving.

Self-Starter Contact Information

Aossey, Nancy | President and CEO, International Medical Corps | International Medical Corps Headquarters, 1919 Santa Monica Blvd., Suite 400, Santa Monica, CA 90404 | P: 310.826.7800 | W: www.InternationalMedicalCorps.org | E: inquiry@International-MedicalCorps.org

Barbaro, Ron D., D.H.L., O. Ont. | Chairman, The Brick Group | The Brick Group, 508 – 4100 Yonge Street, Toronto, ON M2P 2B5 | P: 416.227.0877 | W: www.thebrick.com | E: rbarbaro@thebrick.com

Bensussen, Gale | Chief Executive Officer, Coral Street Partners, LLC | Coral Street Partners, LLC, 365 Twenty Fifth Street, Santa Monica, CA 90402 | P: 310.394.3626 | E: gale@coralstreetpartners.com

Brinton, Roberta Diaz, PhD | R. Pete Vanderveen Chair in Therapeutic Discovery & Development, Professor of Pharmacology & Pharmaceutical Sciences, Biomedical Engineering & Neurology, Norris Foundation Laboratory for Neuroscience Research, and Director of USC's Science, Technology, and Research (STAR) Program | University of Southern California, School of Pharmacy, 1985 Zonal Avenue, Los Angeles, CA 90089 | P: 323.442.1436 | W: http://pharmweb.usc.edu/brinton-lab | E: rbrinton@usc.edu

Burgess, Dr. Gloria J. | President and CEO, Jazz, Inc. | Jazz, Inc., PO Box 777, Edmonds, WA 98020-0777 | P: 206.954.0732 | W: www.gloriaburgess.com | E: Gloria@jazz-inc.com

Camerer, Susan | Executive Director, Vision House | Vision House, PO Box 2951, Renton, WA 98059 | P: 425.228.6356 | W: www. NoHomelessKids.org | E: info@vision-house.org

Campbell, John | Founder, MyVetwork | W: www.myvetwork.com

Campbell, Phyllis J. | Chairman, Pacific Northwest Region, JPMorgan Chase and Co. | JP Morgan Chase and Co., 1301 Second Avenue, Floor 24, Seattle, WA 98101 | W: www.jpmchase.com

Canfield, Jack | The Canfield Companies, The Canfield Training Group | W: www.JackCanfield.com

Cappello, Alexander L. | Chairman and CEO, Cappello Capital Corp. | Cappello Capital Corp., 100 Wilshire Blvd., Suite 1200, Santa Monica, CA 90401 | P: 310.393.6632 | W: www.cappellocorp.com | E: ac@cappellocorp.com

Casey, Kathy | Chef, Mixologist & Entertaining Expert and President, Kathy Casey Food Studios - Liquid Kitchen, Dish D'Lish | Kathy Casey Food Studios - Liquid Kitchen, 5130 Ballard Avenue NW, Seattle, WA 98107 | P: 206.784.7840 | W: www.kathycasey.com | E: info@kathycasey.com

Chou, Helen | President and CEO, Atomic9 | Atomic9, 1617 Cosmo Street, Suite 303, Hollywood, CA 90058 | P: 323.468.6000 | W: www. atomic9.com | E: hchou@atomic9.com

Cook, Sunny Kobe | Customer Experience Consultant, Author/Speaker/ Award-Winning Entrepreneur | Sunny Kobe Cook, PO Box 3771, Seattle, WA 98126 | W: www.SunnyKobeCook.com

Davie, Michael | Documentary Filmmaker | E: Michael@michael-davie.com

Douglas, Tom | W: www.TomDouglas.com

Earl, Joni | Chief Executive Officer, Sound Transit | W: www.soundtran-sit.org

Ellis, James G. | Dean, University of Southern California/Marshall School of Business | W: www.marshall.usc.edu

Europa, Ilona | Singer, Songwriter, Producer, Billboard Charting Artist, Agent for VOX Talent Agency, and Vocal Coach | ILONA EUROPA Productions, 5737 Kanan Road, Suite 237, Agoura Hills, CA 91301 | P: 805.338.4592 | W: www.myspace.com/ILONAEUROPA, www. ILONAEUROPA.com, www.VOXUSA.net | E: ILONAeuropa@ gmail.com

Geller, Dan | Producer and Director, Geller/Goldfine Productions | W: www.gellergoldfine.com

Goldfine, Dayna | Producer and Director, Geller/Goldfine Productions | Geller/Goldfine Productions, 930 Pierce Street, San Francisco, CA 94115 | P: 415.440.3301 | W: www.gellergoldfine.com | E: Dayna@ gellergoldfine.com

Greenberg, Jared | Co-Founder, Somaly Mam Foundation | Somaly Mam Foundation, PO Box 4569, New York, NY 10163 | W: www. somaly.org

Gunvalson, Victoria Lynn (Vicki) | President and Owner, Coto Insurance & Financial Services, Inc. | Coto Insurance & Financial Services, 30212 Tomas, Suite 110, Rancho Santa Margarita, CA 92688 | P: 949.858.7200 | W: www.vickigunvalson.com | E: vicki@ cotoinsurance.com

Haden, Pat | Athletic Director, University of Southern California

Himonidis, Stephanie ("Chiquibaby") | Television and Radio personality, UNIVISION | P: 619.307.4922 | W: www.chiquibaby.com | E: viva@chiquibaby.com

Karch, Megan | CEO, FareStart | FareStart, 700 Virginia Street, Seattle, WA 98101 | P: 206.443.1233 | W: www.farestart.org | E: megan@ farestart.org

Lam, Wing G. | Co-Founder, Wahoo's Fish Taco | Wahoo's Fish Taco, 2855 Pullman Street, Santa Ana, CA 92705 | P: 949.222.0670 | W: www.wahoos.com | E: wing.lam@wahoos.com

Lepore, Debra Facktor | President, DFL Space LLC and Executive Director, Stevens Institute of Technology | DFL Space LLC, 824 – 170th Place NE, Bellevue, WA 98008 | P: 425.985.1350 | W: www.DFLspace.com | E: debra@DFLspace.com

Loaiza, David | VP, Quantitative Research, JP Morgan Chase | E: david07jesse@gmail.com

Nguyen, Quy ("Q") | CEO, Allyance Communications, Inc. | Allyance Communications, Inc., 2485 McCabe Way, Suite 100, Irvine, CA 92614 | P: 949.863.0025 | W: www.allyance.net | E: info@allyance.net

Pappas, Lori J. | Founder and President, Global Team for Local Initiatives | Global Team for Local Initiatives, PO Box 11277, Bainbridge Island, WA 98110 | P: 206.780.4353 | W: www.gtli.us | E: info@gtli.us

Pascal, Patrick | President, Chelsea Management Company | Chelsea Management Company, 444 South Flower Street, Suite 2340, Los Angeles, CA 90071 | P: 213.362.9200 | W: www.chelseamanagement.com

Prentice, Arlen I. (Arnie) | Chairman, Kibble & Prentice, a USI Company | Kibble & Prentice, 601 Union Street, Suite 1000, Seattle, WA 98101 | P: 206.441.6300 | W: www.kpcom.com

Rahn, Mikala L., PhD | President and Founder, Public *Works*, Inc./ Learning *Works!* Charter School | Public *Works*, Inc., 90 North Daisy Avenue, Pasadena, CA 91107 | P: 626.564.9890 | W: www.publicworksinc.org | E: mikala@publicworksinc.org

Robertson, Jon H. | Dean, Lynn University Conservatory of Music | Lynn University, 3601 North Military Trail, Boca Raton, FL 33431 | P: 561.237.7701 | W: www.lynn.edu/music | E: jrobertson@lynn.edu

Ruffner, Ginny | Artist, Ginny Ruffner Studio | W: www.ginnyruffner. com | E: ginny@ginnyruffner.com

Sabey, Dave | President, Sabey Corporation | Sabey Corporation, 12201 Tukwila International Blvd., Seattle, WA 98168 | P: 206.281.8700 | W: www.sabey.com

Sanchez, Ricardo E. | Vice President, Communications and Educational Services, SeaMar Community Health Centers | SeaMar Community Health Centers, 1040 South Henderson Street, Seattle, WA 98108 | P: 206.763.5277 | W: www.seamarchc.org | E: ricardosanchez@ seamarchc.org

Sapp, Jeffrey K., Captain, U.S. Navy (Retired), MS, MA, MA | Founder and President, J.K. Sapp Enterprises, LLC – Motivational Speaking for Business Improvement, Leadership, & Personal Development | J.K. Sapp Enterprises, LLC, 7425 Evington Drive, Suite 301, Warrenton, VA 20187 | P: 703.955.2393 | W: www.JKSapp.com | E: JKSapp@JKSapp.com

Schwartz, Pepper, PhD | Professor of Sociology, University of Washington, Chief Expert of PerfectMatch.com, and AARP Love and Relationships Ambassador | University of Washington, Department of Sociology, Box 353340, Seattle, WA 98195 | W: www.drpepperschwartz.com | E: pepperschwartz@hotmail.com

Smart, Phil M., Sr. | Phil Smart Mercedes-Benz | P: 206.324.5959 | W: www.philsmart.com

Smulyan, Jeffrey H. (Jeff) | Chairman and CEO, Emmis Communications | Emmis Communications, 40 Monument Circle, Suite 700, Indianapolis, IN 46204 | P: 317.266.0100 | W: www.Emmis.com | E: jeff@emmis.com

Stack, Geoffrey | Managing Director, SARES-REGIS Group | SARES-REGIS Group, 18802 Bardeen Avenue, Irvine, CA 92612 | P: 949.756.5959 | W: www.SARES-REGIS.com

Staheli, Lana, PhD | Bounce Be Transformed | P: 206.525.4204 | W: www.bouncebetransformed.com | E: lanastaheli@gmail.com

Stowell, Kent & Francia Russell | Founding Artistic Directors, Pacific Northwest Ballet | Pacific Northwest Ballet, 301 Mercer Street, Seattle, WA 98109 | P: 206.441.9411 | W: www.pnb.org

Tice, Louis E. (Lou) | Chairman, The Pacific Institute | W: www.thepacificinstitute.com

Todd, Jonathan | Owner, Jonathan Todd Management & Marketing, Jonathan Todd Artist Management, Director of Marketing & Management, ICONDUIT, New Media Management | Jonathan Todd Management & Marketing, 5737 Kanan Road, Suite 237, Agoura Hills, CA 91301 | P: 310.929.0771 | W: www.iconduit.biz, www.CertifiedRatings.com | E: StarManager@me.com

Ukropina, Rob R. | Managing Partner, Black Diamond Ventures | Black Diamond Ventures, 500 Newport Center Drive, Suite 580, Newport Beach, CA 92660 | P: 949.644.4288 | W: www.bdventures.com | E: rob@bdventures.com

Walsh, Bob | President and CEO, One World 2011 | W: www.oneworld2011.org

KEYFACTS ABOUT OUR AMAZING SELF-STARTERS

Name of Self-Starter	Birth Order?	Extrovert or Introvert?	Left- or Right-Handed?
	1st Generation American?	Planner or Procrastinator?	Lead with Head or Heart?
Aossey, Nancy	Second born of four	Extrovert	Right
	Both parents–1st generation	Planner	Head
Barbaro, Ron	Middle child	Extrovert	Left
	Canadian	Planner; definitely not a procrastinator	Heart
Bensussen, Gale	Only child	Introvert who likes to be social	Right
	No	Planner	Heart
Brinton, Roberta Diaz	Second born of four (Older twin)	Extrovert, with contemplative introversion capability	Right
	Mother–1st generation	Both	Both
Burgess, Gloria	Middle child	Introvert	Right
	No	Procrastinator	Heart
Camerer, Susan	Third born of four	Introvert, although pretends to be extrovert	Right
	Father born in Holland	Planner	Heart, in an analytical way
Campbell, John	Firstborn	Introvert	Right
	No	Procrastinator	Heart

Name of Self-Starter	Birth Order?	Extrovert or Introvert?	Left- or Right-Handed?
	1st Generation American?	Planner or Procrastinator?	Lead with Head or Heart?
Campbell, Phyllis	Firstborn of five	Extrovert, but needs quiet time	Right
	No	Planner	Head and heart
Canfield, Jack	Firstborn	Introvert when younger; now more of an extrovert, depending on situation	Right
	No	Voracious planner	Heart
Cappello, Alex	Firstborn of four	Both	Right
	Both parents–1st generation	Procrastinator at times; planner when important	Heart
Casey, Kathy	Only child (Adopted)	Extrovert	Right, but left for golf and bowling
	Both birth parents–1st generation Adoptive mom–Canadian	Super planner maniac	Always leads with heart
Chou, Helen	Youngest of two	Extrovert	Right
	Both parents–1st generation	Planner	Heart first, but the head follows right behind
Cook, Sunny Kobe	Youngest of two	Conscious extrovert	Right
	No	Both, and meticulously organized	Heart, except in business, then head

| Name of Self-Starter | Birth Order? | Extrovert or Introvert? | Left- or Right-Handed? |
	1st Generation American?	Planner or Procrastinator?	Lead with Head or Heart?
Davie, Michael	Firstborn	Extrovert until recently; now quieter	Right
	Born in Zimbabwe	Both, and meticulous planner when necessary	Heart
Douglas, Tom	Middle child	Extrovert	Right
	No	Procrastinator	Head
Earl, Joni	Youngest of three	Extrovert	Right
	Father born in England	Either; depends on circumstances	Head with heart
Ellis, Jim	Firstborn of three	Extrovert	Used to be right, but now left, since nerve affliction
	No	Procrastinator earlier in life; now a planner	Heart
Europa, Ilona	Youngest of two	Extrovert	Right
	Born in Poland	Both	Heart first, head second
Geller, Dan	Firstborn	Extrovert	Right
	No	Planner	Heart
Goldfine, Dayna	Firstborn	Extrovert	Right
	No	Both	Heart

Name of Self-Starter	Birth Order?	Extrovert or Introvert?	Left- or Right-Handed?
	1st Generation American?	Planner or Procrastinator?	Lead with Head or Heart?
Greenberg, Jared	Youngest of two	Probably extrovert but not in an extreme manner	Right
	No	Planner	Head
Gunvalson, Vicki	Middle child of five	Extrovert	Right
	No	Planner	Head
Haden, Pat	Fourth out of five	Was introvert; now an extrovert	Right
	No	Planner	Heart
Himonidis, Stephanie	Firstborn of two	Extrovert	Right
	Born in Mexico	Both	Heart
Karch, Megan	Youngest of three	Both; tries to be more extroverted	Right
	No	Procrastinator	Heart, but very analytical
Lam, Wing	Middle child of five	Used to be introvert, now extrovert	Right
	Yes	Procrastinator	Heart, passion
Lepore, Debra Facktor	Firstborn	Extrovert	Right
	Father–1st generation	Both, depending on situation	Depends, both

| Name of Self-Starter | Birth Order? | Extrovert or Introvert? | Left- or Right-Handed? |
	1st Generation American?	Planner or Procrastinator?	Lead with Head or Heart?
Loaiza, David	Firstborn of second marriage	Extrovert	Right
	Born in Bolivia	Planner	Head, heart with certain decisions
Nguyen, Quy	Second born	Extrovert	Right
	Born in Vietnam	Planner	Heart
Pappas, Lori	Youngest of four	Naturally an introvert, but Myers-Briggs results indicate both	Right
	Father born in Greece	Procrastinator	Head first
Pascal, Patrick	Third born	Extrovert	Right
	Born in Ireland	Both	Has to be a combination but I lead with my head
Prentice, Arnie	Oldest son	Extrovert	Right
	No	Planner	Heart
Rahn, Mikala	Firstborn	Professionally an extrovert; personally introverted	Right
	Yes	Planner by nature	Heart

Name of Self-Starter	Birth Order?	Extrovert or Introvert?	Left- or Right-Handed?
	1st Generation American?	Planner or Procrastinator?	Lead with Head or Heart?
Robertson, Jon	Youngest of four	Introvert by nature; extrovert because of profession	Right
	Yes	Planner when it comes to work; procrastinator by nature	Heart
Ruffner, Ginny	Firstborn	Extrovert	Right now; left before accident
	No	Planner	Head
Sabey, Dave	Middle child of three	Introvert, but most people think he's an extrovert	Left
	Mother–1st generation	Action-oriented and partial planner	They are hooked together
Sanchez, Ricardo	Youngest of seven	Extrovert	Right
	Yes	Both	Heart
Sapp, Jeffrey	Youngest of four	Introverted extrovert	Both
	No	Procrastinating planner	Heart, but depends on situation
Schwartz, Pepper	Youngest child	Extrovert	Right
	Both parents–1st generation	Planner usually, but procrastinates with some things	Heart, but head isn't far behind

Name of Self-Starter	Birth Order?	Extrovert or Introvert?	Left- or Right-Handed?
	1st Generation American?	Planner or Procrastinator?	Lead with Head or Heart?
Smart, Phil	Oldest child	Extrovert who doesn't get along well with introverts	Right
	No	Planner	Heart
Smulyan, Jeff	Middle child of three	Extrovert	Right, although left for golf and baseball
	No	Both	Heart
Stack, Jeff	Firstborn of two	Extrovert although introvert at times	Right
	No	Planner	Head
Staheli, Lana	Oldest child	Extrovert, more than some people and less than others	Right
	No	Planner	Head
Stowell, Kent & Russell, Francia	Second born/ Firstborn	Extrovert/ Introvert	Right/Right
	Mother–1st generation/ Both parents–1st generation	Both/Both	Heart/Head
Tice, Lou	Second born	A little of both	Right
	No	Both	Changed to heart in recent years

| Name of Self-Starter | Birth Order? | Extrovert or Introvert? | Left- or Right-Handed? |
	1st Generation American?	Planner or Procrastinator?	Lead with Head or Heart?
Todd, Jonathan	Firstborn of two	Extrovert	Right
	Father—1st generation	Both	Heart
Ukropina, Rob	Third born of four	Extrovert times 10	Right
	No	Planner	Heart
Walsh, Bob	Youngest of two	Extrovert	Right
	Both parents—1st generation	Procrastinator; definitely not a planner	Heart

About the Author

Dr. Julie Miller

The old adage "It takes one to know one" certainly holds true in this book, as author Julie Miller is, herself, the epitome of a self-starter. Having met many during her travels as a speaker and consultant to numerous Fortune 500 companies, she can spot a self-starter from a mile away.

This isn't surprising, since her credentials reflect both a strong academic background—including a doctorate degree in leadership studies—and real life, practical experience gained while training and consulting with more than 600,000 business professionals.

As Julie studied a variety of successful self-starters, she noticed that most of them possessed such classic characteristics as perseverance or creativity or a passion for a specific vision of their future. But what if there was more to it than that? What set those individuals apart? To find the answer, she interviewed dozens of self-starters. She dug deeper and discovered it's actually a combination of traits and attitudes, or *traititudes*, that—when combined with other factors—were what sky-rocketed these individuals to the top of their game.

"The main difference is these people got up, got going and got on with it," Julie explained. "They took action. They figured it out, and when they couldn't do even that much, they still took one small step in what felt like the right direction at the time—and often was."

But *how* they move forward is as unique to each person as a fingerprint. Their own blend and balance of *traititudes* capitalize on their skills and minimize their weaknesses. Self-starters aren't perfect people, Julie realized; they just know who they are and what they want. And they keep moving, going and getting . . . until they arrive.

Julie lives in Seattle, Washington, with her family, although she regularly travels across the country or internationally to deliver keynote speeches or give workshop sessions.

You may contact her at www.SuccessFactorsInc.net
Julie@DrJulieMiller.com
Or contact her directly at:
SuccessFactorsInc.Net
425.485.3221

GET STARTED!

Congratulations—you've actually already begun. After reading these forty-eight self-starters' inspiring stories, you've realized you, too, can acquire and grow your own *traititude* to kick-start your success.

Or, maybe, your self-starter plans are well underway, yet these nine traits intrigue you. Which ones would work best for you? Learning more about them could be all you need to ramp up your current efforts and reach a higher, more fulfilling level.

Because each self-starter's journey is as unique as the set of experiences and *traititudes* that make up that person, you may want some guidance—some outside expertise and inspiration—to help you discover and clarify your own path.

Dr. Julie will ignite the self-starter in you!

Learn how to use these nine traits in your own life. Get up and get going—take action. Dr. Julie will share proven tips and ideas to help you uncover and practice your own *traititude*—and stay on track.

Do you have a group of people who are itching to make their dreams come true? If so, Dr. Julie is an experienced speaker, keynoter and seminar presenter who has helped more than 600,000 people—including those at numerous top Fortune 500 companies—improve the quality of their lives.

Visit Dr. Julie online at her Secrets of Self-Starters blog and website:

www.SuccessFactorsInc.net
Julie@DrJulieMiller.com
Or contact her directly at:
SuccessFactorsInc.Net
425.485.3221